102 Days of War

DAYS OF WAR

How Osama bin Laden, al Qaeda & the Taliban Survived 2001

Yaniv Barzilai

Foreword by BRUCE RIEDEL

Potomac Books
Washington, D.C.

Map 3, "The Horse Soldiers' Ride to Mazar-i-Sharif, October 19–November 10, 2001,"
reprinted by permission of International Creative Management; copyright © Doug
Stanton, *Horse Soldiers: The Extraordinary Story of a Band of U.S. Soldiers Who Rode to
Victory in Afghanistan* (New York: Scribner, 2009).

Map 6, "Map Carried by Dalton Fury," reprinted by permission of Dalton Fury; copyright
© Dalton Fury, *Kill Bin Laden: A Delta Force Commander's Account of the Hunt for the
World's Most Wanted Man* (New York: St. Martin's, 2008).

All statements of fact, opinion, or analysis expressed are those of the author and do not
reflect the official positions or views of any U.S. Government agency. Nothing in the
contents should be construed as asserting or implying U.S. Government authentication of
information or endorsement of the author's views. This material has been reviewed by the
U.S. Government to prevent the disclosure of classified information.

Library of Congress Cataloging-in-Publication Data
Barzilai, Yaniv
    102 days of war : how Osama bin Laden, al Qaeda & the Taliban survived 2001 / Yaniv
Barzilai : foreword by Bruce Riedel. — 1st edition.
        p. cm.
    Includes bibliographical references and index.
    ISBN 978-1-61234-533-8 (hbk. : alk. paper)
    ISBN 978-1-61234-534-5 (electronic)
    1. Operation Enduring Freedom, 2001– 2. Taliban. 3. Bin Laden, Osama, 1957–2011.
4. Tora Bora, Battle of, Afghanistan, 2001. 5. War on Terrorism, 2001–2009. 6. National
security—United States—Decision making. 7. Command of troops—Case studies. 8.
Afghanistan—History, Military—21st century. 9. United States—History, Military—21st
century. I. Title.
    DS371.4.B38 2013
    958.104'7—dc23

                                                            2012047589

Printed in the United States of America on acid-free paper that meets the American
National Standards Institute Z39-48 Standard.

Potomac Books
22841 Quicksilver Drive
Dulles, Virginia 20166

First Edition

10 9 8 7 6 5 4 3 2 1

To those who serve,
and to the people of Afghanistan
whose lives have been destroyed by
three decades of war

CONTENTS

MAPS

AUTHOR'S NOTE

102 Days of War went through an exhaustive eleven-month pre-publication review by the Department of State, Department of Defense, Central Intelligence Agency, and White House National Security Staff in order to prevent the disclosure of classified information. As the chapter on sources and methodology describes, all information for this book was derived from open sources or on-the-record interviews.

Nevertheless, seven thematic features were deemed classified and therefore have been removed from the book. None of the removed information was critical to the narrative; indeed, most of the redacted material concerns mundane information readily available in the public domain. For example, the Defense Department redacted unit names from the U.S. Special Operations community that, while technically classified, have been known publicly for years. These include the Navy SEAL team that conducted the raid on the bin Laden compound in Abbottabad and the Army Special Operations commando unit of which Dalton Fury, the author of *Kill Bin Laden: A Delta Force Commander's Account of the Hunt for the World's Most Wanted Man*, was a member.

Managing the U.S. government's pre-publication review proved to be a tremendous challenge. Initially, the Central Intelligence Agency and Defense Department redacted information in nearly one hundred places. The CIA's Publication Review Board issued dozens of redactions but withdrew practically all of its objections upon considering an appeal. The Defense Department issued fifty-eight redactions on thirty-five pages to protect five thematic features from disclosure and ultimately upheld all redactions after a lengthy appeals process. These five pieces of information can be found in speeches from defense secretaries during their time in office, in the memoirs of four-star generals, on the Defense Department website, in official U.S. military histories, or in a copy of my undergraduate honors thesis available at the University of North Carolina's Wilson library, but in accordance with the Defense Department's directive you will not find them in this book. I have chosen to use alternative language in three of the five instances and have deleted the other two in their entirety in order to minimize damage to the narrative while complying with the Defense Department's decision.

In the end, the pre-publication review delayed the release of *102 Days of War* by eight months and threatened to fundamentally distort the narrative. As an American diplomat, I strongly believe in the obligation to protect all classified information. But at the same time I believe that rigorous historical scholarship is a universal good that can inform leaders about difficult decisions and help them avoid the mistakes of the past. In that regard, the U.S. government also has a keen interest in encouraging its employees to read and write about history. And who better to do so than the military officers, defense officials, intelligence professionals, and diplomats who are on the front lines of America's foreign policy and national security every day? Of course, sensitive and classified topics must be vigorously safeguarded, but the U.S. government needs to strike a better balance between protecting information and encouraging scholarly activities in the public domain. The pre-publication review process remains too arbitrary, lengthy, and disjointed to allow most government professionals to engage in scholarly activities that benefit the national security community and the broader public.

FOREWORD

On September 11, 2001, I was in the White House Situation Room when the first news of the attack on the World Trade Center was received. As special assistant to the president and senior director for Near East and North African affairs, I would be a firsthand witness to the attack on our country and the counterattack in Afghanistan ordered by President George W. Bush. I have had the privilege to serve four presidents on the staff of the National Security Council over almost twenty years, but no moments were as dramatic and important as that fall day and the hundred days that followed.

The White House and Washington felt under siege during those days. No one knew whether another devastating attack was coming. For a time it appeared our foreign enemy was already sending deadly anthrax-filled letter bombs to Washington, and only later did it become clear the culprit was a deranged American. Threats of new attacks flooded the intelligence community. While the country rallied behind President Bush, it was anxious and frightened.

The response to the attacks of September 11 was inevitably going to reflect the crisis atmosphere that gripped the nation. It was clear within hours of the attack that al Qaeda and Osama bin Laden were responsible; it was also clear that there was no war plan on the shelf to go after their base in Afghanistan. The Pentagon was not ready to begin a war on the other side of the world in a landlocked, remote nation. The CIA fortunately had assets and contacts and some plans, but the CIA is not responsible for war planning, diplomacy, or nation-building. The Bush team had to put together a response under fire; inevitably it would be improvised, confused, and incomplete. That some members of the team were more fixated on Iraq than Afghanistan only made it all the more difficult.

This brilliant book chronicles the result. Yaniv Barzilai, a graduate student of mine at the Johns Hopkins University School of Advanced International Studies (SAIS), interviewed many of the key actors in the American response to 9/11 and has put together an insightful narrative of those 102 days between the attack and the end of the Battle of Tora Bora in December 2001, which completed major military operations. It is an especially important story since the Afghan war did not end in 2001; it has become America's longest war ever. Why it did not end a decade ago is vitally important today.

The first 102 days of the war did produce a brilliant victory in one sense. With very few American casualties and relatively small resources, the CIA and the American military toppled the Islamic Emirate of Afghanistan and ousted the Taliban regime that had protected al Qaeda. Al Qaeda's state within a state and its terrorist camps were destroyed. But it was also a failure. Bin Laden, his deputy and heir Ayman al-Zawahiri, and Taliban leader Mullah Mohammed Omar all successfully escaped from the American chase into Pakistan. Within a year, in November 2002, bin Laden would reappear in an audio message taking credit for inspiring a new mass-casualty terror attack in Indonesia that killed 202 Indonesians, Australians, and others, and promising more attacks would come. We now know that he would live another nine years before the CIA would find him in a hideout in Abbottabad, Pakistan.

Yaniv's remarkable book demonstrates that bin Laden's escape was the product of more than his own planning and good fortune. The confused thinking in the White House and Pentagon about war aims, strategy, and goals that marked the 102 days led to poorly resourced efforts to hunt down the al Qaeda leadership in 2001. They then led to poorly constructed efforts to restore stability in Afghanistan and to the revival of the Taliban. A war that should have ended in triumph and a stable Afghanistan drifted into an open-ended insurgency with no end in sight. Confusion over what we needed to accomplish in Afghanistan was evident from the beginning of the war and prevented our commanders on the ground from achieving all that they could have. That confusion and drift started at the top in the White House.

The story also sets the stage for understanding our ongoing dysfunctional relationship with Pakistan, a country of far more strategic importance than its neighbor. The Bush team rightly saw the importance of Pakistan to the war effort against al Qaeda, but it seemed unable to grasp how Islamabad intended to hedge its bets from the beginning and retain its ties to the Taliban and other extremists. This book chronicles Pakistan's efforts to assist the retreat of the Taliban and to keep its options open. The seeds of future trouble began in 2001 and would lead to the extraordinary decision of President Barack Obama in 2011 not to share any information on our plans to bring justice to bin Laden in Abbottabad. Obama had learned the lesson of 2001 not to rely on Pakistan to fight al Qaeda.

This book explains in detail how al Qaeda survived in 2001. We may never unravel all the mysteries of those 102 days. Bin Laden took some of them to his grave in the Arabian Sea. Others are still concealed in the archives of the Pakistani intelligence service. But *102 Days of War* is an essential book that provides the best account by far of what happened that fall and why. It is also a major contribution to understanding the leadership strengths and weaknesses of a presidency under siege.

BRUCE RIEDEL
senior fellow at the Brookings Institution
author of *The Search for al Qaeda: Its Leadership, Ideology, and Future*
and *Deadly Embrace: Pakistan, America, and the Future of the Global Jihad*

PREFACE

War is a vital matter of the state. It is the field on which life or death
is determined and the road that leads to either survival or ruin, and
must be examined with the greatest care.

— SUN TZU, THE ART OF WARFARE[1]

102 Days of War is based on interviews with thirteen U.S. officials who presided over
the U.S. war in Afghanistan at every level. The following individuals (with their posi-
tions at the time indicated) were interviewed for this book: from the White House,
National Security Advisor Condoleezza Rice, Deputy National Security Advisor
Stephen Hadley, and National Security Council Director for Southwest Asia Amb.
Zalmay Khalilzad; from the Department of Defense, Under Secretary of Defense for
Policy Douglas Feith; from the U.S. military, Chairman of the Joint Chiefs of Staff
Gen. Richard Myers, the commander of the Fifth Special Forces Group Col. John
Mulholland, the commander of Task Force 58 Brig. Gen. James Mattis, and "Dalton
Fury," the commander of the Army special operations team at Tora Bora and the
author of *Kill Bin Laden: A Delta Force Commander's Account of the Hunt for the World's
Most Wanted Man*; from the State Department, Deputy Secretary of State Richard
Armitage and Special Representative to the Afghan Opposition Amb. James Dobbins;
from the Central Intelligence Agency, Deputy Director of Central Intelligence John
McLaughlin, CIA field commander Gary Berntsen, and CIA analyst Michael
Scheuer. Pulitzer Prize–winning authors Dexter Filkins and Steve Coll also partic-
ipated in interviews for this book. Direct quotes have been provided as often as
possible in order to preserve the words of these individuals in their original form.

In addition to these interviews, *102 Days of War* makes extensive use of memoirs, official histories, and secondary sources available as of April 2012. Nonetheless, few official U.S. documents have been declassified, leaving a gaping hole in the record for future historians. Readers further interested in the sources and methodology behind this book should refer to the "Sources and Methodology" section following the epilogue.

One important aspect of the American response to the terrorist attacks of September 11, 2001, that *102 Days of War* does not further address is the emotional and psychological impact that they had on the nation's leadership. September 11 was an immensely traumatic and devastating event for the leaders responsible for America's national security. Most of the officials described in this book visited the sites of the attacks while the wreckage was still smoldering. Many of these leaders knew people who died in the attacks, and many more met with families of the victims. The attacks were deeply personal for those in charge of the U.S. government. I therefore encourage readers to empathize with these individuals, who almost certainly must have been overwhelmed by feelings of sadness, anger, responsibility, courage, fear, and guilt. To speculate as to how the emotional and psychological impact of 9/11 affected specific aspects of the campaign is beyond the scope of this book. However, this impact nevertheless represents a notable undercurrent of the first 102 days of war.

At the conclusion of my interview with former under secretary of defense Feith, I asked him to sign my copy of his book. After wishing me the best of luck on my research, he chose to quote former defense secretary Donald Rumsfeld and wrote, "Above all, precision." I have heeded these words closely. Indeed, I have gone through extensive measures to ensure that *102 Days of War* is true to the available evidence. From fact-checking to cross-referencing to asking the individuals I interviewed to corroborate unclear or dubious evidence, I have done my best to provide the reader with a precise and accurate narrative of the events that occurred between September 11 and December 22, 2001. I have worked hard to avoid political partisanship in this book. I have also made no attempts to appease my sources or portray them in anything other than an objective manner.

As always, historical scholarship is limited by the sources available; *102 Days of War* is by no means a definitive account. Rather, it unites the disparate but salient aspects of Operation Enduring Freedom into a cogent historical narrative. Any errors are my own.

INTRODUCTION

In the aftermath of the September 11, 2001, terrorist attacks, the United States of America scrambled to retaliate against an obscure enemy in a distant land. Instead of following a predictable and conventional approach to war, the architects of Operation Enduring Freedom developed a creative strategy for the war in Afghanistan that paired unconventional warfare with advanced technologies to strengthen friendly indigenous forces. In doing so, America bypassed the need for a long, massive buildup of troops in a theater of conflict known for its challenging terrain and proclivity for expelling foreign aggressors. The strategy developed for Operation Enduring Freedom relied on a small number of special operations forces (SOF), combined with Central Intelligence Agency (CIA) paramilitary officers and the might of U.S. airpower, to bolster the Afghan opposition, topple the Taliban, and disrupt al Qaeda. As each of these elements of national power integrated into the war effort, an innovative model of warfare emerged in apparent contrast to its predecessors.

In the words of President George W. Bush, America fought "a different kind of war."[1] This new strategy enabled the United States to respond in a rapid manner with surprisingly few American troops. Nonetheless, the strategy faced considerable impediments to its success. The 9/11 attacks caught the U.S. armed forces vastly unprepared. Without an off-the-shelf war plan for Afghanistan or intelligence on the enemy, the American military struggled to develop an adequate war plan for an adversary who was not confined to national borders. The CIA possessed most of the knowledge and expertise on Afghanistan and al Qaeda in the American government and acted as a pivotal intermediary between the U.S. military and Afghan resistance forces. But poor weather conditions and the military's institutional aversion to risk delayed the insertion of troops into Afghanistan. Combined with a lack of actionable intelligence and salient targets, the difficulty in deploying American forces into landlocked Afghanistan generated an initial operational impasse.

A strategic void further limited the effectiveness of the campaign, as the chaotic war-planning process failed to differentiate between removing Afghanistan as a sanctuary for terrorist organizations and decisively destroying al Qaeda. Competing visions of objectives were not resolved before the campaign began. Operations were structured around toppling the Taliban first and then expelling al Qaeda from Afghanistan. While the president and his cabinet were eager to eliminate al Qaeda and do so quickly, they nonetheless failed to establish and formalize the destruction of al Qaeda as an objective for the impending war. Many variables in a complex and changing operational environment contributed to the eventual failure to decimate al Qaeda in the attack on Afghanistan, but the lack of clarity about American goals represented the largest limiting factor in eliminating the terrorist organization.

The initial operational impasse broke when the White House agreed to unleash the Northern Alliance by shifting American air assets from bombing strategic targets to close air support. In November this multiethnic organization of anti-Taliban groups swiftly defeated the Taliban in most of the major cities in Afghanistan. In a matter of days, the Northern Alliance went from occupying 15 percent of Afghanistan to controlling half the country.

However, the United States missed the best opportunity to destroy al Qaeda's leadership and kill bin Laden in early December at the Battle of Tora Bora in the mountains of eastern Afghanistan. Fewer than one hundred Western commandos supported a coalition of unreliable Afghan warlords in attacking al Qaeda's most prominent stronghold and the location of Osama bin Laden. The battle forced hundreds—if not thousands—of al Qaeda and Taliban fighters to retreat across the border into Pakistan, thus fulfilling the U.S. objective of removing Afghanistan as a haven for al Qaeda. But without adequately sealing the border to prevent their escape, the United States ensured the survival of Osama bin Laden and al Qaeda.

The Battle of Tora Bora was the largest failure of the campaign. Contrary to conventional wisdom, it was not just a failure in tactics that allowed bin Laden to escape and al Qaeda to survive. The reliance on dubious Afghan allies, the insufficient number of American troops, and the inability to seal the border contributed to the eventual outcome at Tora Bora but did not wholly determine it. Indeed, the lack of success in the Battle of Tora Bora was as much the product of failures in policy and leadership as it was of tactical mistakes. By instructing the military to remove Afghanistan as a sanctuary for al Qaeda, the civilian leadership in the White House designated the expulsion of al Qaeda—and not its destruction—as the central U.S. objective. And while the battle raged in the mountains of Tora Bora, President Bush and Defense Secretary Donald Rumsfeld remained aloof from the entirety of the engagement and relinquished responsibility to Gen. Tommy Franks, the commander of the U.S. Central Command (CENTCOM). In the end, the failure by America's civilian leadership to intervene in the affairs of the U.S. military during the Battle of Tora Bora amounted to a dereliction of duty.

Many consider the defeat of the Taliban ten weeks after September 11 to be evidence of the success of Operation Enduring Freedom.[2] Others consider the plan imperfect for its failure to destroy and defeat al Qaeda.[3] In reality, the 102 days following the September 11, 2001, terrorist attacks saw neither decisive success nor a fundamentally flawed effort. Rather, a series of operational and policy miscalculations reduced the effectiveness of a brilliant and creative plan of attack. The strategy pursued for the opening campaign of Operation Enduring Freedom removed the Taliban from power and disrupted al Qaeda in Afghanistan but ultimately failed to achieve what should have been the primary objective of destroying al Qaeda. This is the story of the operational victories and strategic defeats that transpired after the calm, clear morning of September 11, 2001, gave way to 102 days of war.

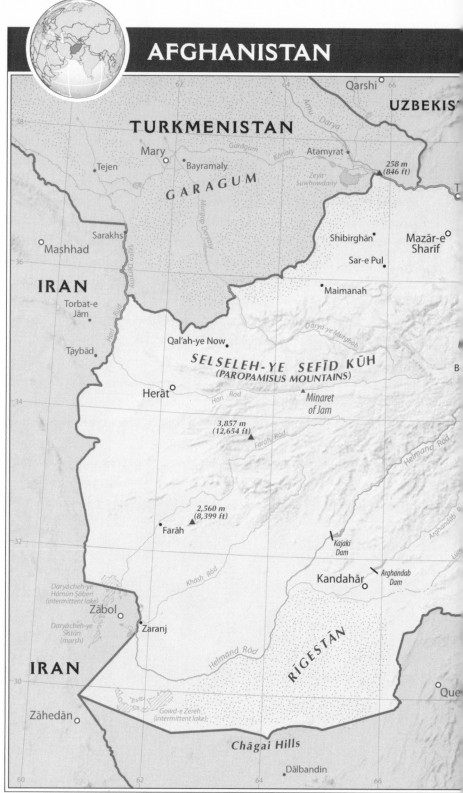

Qarshi

UZBEKIS'

TURKMENISTAN

Amu Darya

Mary

Bayramaly

Atamyrat

Tejen

Gardgum

Kanaly

GARAGUM

Zeyit Suwhowdany

258 m (846 ft)

T

Murgap Deryasy

Sarakhs

Shibirghān

Mazār-e Sharīf

Mashhad

Sar-e Pul

IRAN

Tejen Deryasy

Hari Rud

Torbat-e Jām

Maimanah

Tāybād

Daryā-ye Murghāb

Qal'ah-ye Now

SELSELEH-YE SEFĪD KŪH
(PAROPAMISUS MOUNTAINS)

Herāt

Hari Rōd

Minaret of Jam

Helmand Rōd

3,857 m (12,654 ft)

Farāh Rōd

Arghandāb Rōd

2,560 m (8,399 ft)

Farāh

Kajaki Dam

B

Khāsh Rōd

Kandahār

Arghandab Dam

Lur

Daryācheh-ye Hāmūn Şāberi (intermittent lake)

Zābol

Daryācheh-ye Sīstān (marsh)

Zaranj

RĪGESTĀN

IRAN

Helmand Rōd

Que

Zāhedān

Gowd-e Zereh (intermittent lake)

Chāgai Hills

Dālbandin

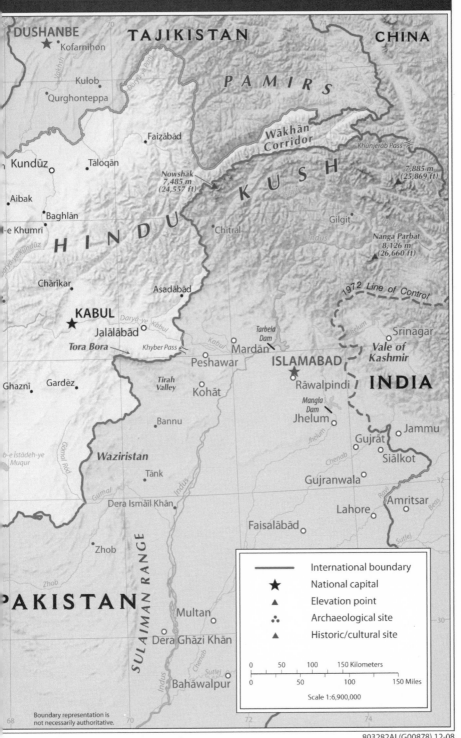

DUSHANBE
Kofarnihon

TAJIKISTAN

CHINA

Kulob

Qurghonteppa

P A M I R S

Faizābād

Wākhān
Corridor

Khunjerab Pass

Kundūz

Tāloqān

Nowshāk
7,485 m
(24,557 ft)

K U S H

7,885 m
(25,869 ft)

Aibak

Baghlān

-e Khumri

H I N D U

Chitrāl

Gilgit

Indus

Nanga Parbat
8,126 m
(26,660 ft)

Chārīkar

Asadābād

1972 Line of Control

Srinagar

KABUL
Jalālābād

Darya-ye Kabul

Tarbela
Dam

Vale of
Kashmir

Tora Bora

Khyber Pass

Mardān

Kabul

ISLAMABAD

Peshawar

Rāwalpindi

INDIA

Ghaznī

Gardēz

Tirah
Valley

Kohāt

Mangla
Dam

Jhelum

Jammu

Bannu

Jhelum

Gujrāt

Gujrānwāla

Siālkot

b-e Istādeh-ye
Muqur

Waziristan

Tānk

Indus

Chenab

32

Dera Ismāīl Khān

Gumal

Lahore

Amritsar

Zhob

Faisalābād

Beas

Ravi

PAKISTAN

SULAIMAN RANGE

Multan

Sutlej

30

Dera Ghāzi Khān

Chenab

Sutlej

Bahāwalpur

	International boundary
★	National capital
▲	Elevation point
∴	Archaeological site
▲	Historic/cultural site

0   50   100   150 Kilometers
0   50   100   150 Miles

Scale 1:6,900,000

68   70   72   74

ABBREVIATIONS

AIA	Afghan Interim Authority
CENTCOM	United States Central Command
CIA	Central Intelligence Agency
CSAR	combat search and rescue
CTC	CIA Counterterrorism Center
CTC/SO	CIA Counterterrorism Center Special Operations
DIA	Defense Intelligence Agency
DOD	Department of Defense
ISI	Pakistan's Inter-Services Intelligence
JCS	Joint Chiefs of Staff
JDAM	Joint Direct Attack Munitions
JeM	Jaish-e-Mohammed
K2	Karshi Khanabad, Uzbekistan
MSS	mission support site
NMCC	National Military Command Center
NSC	National Security Council
ODA	Operational Detachment Alpha
OPLAN	operations plan
QDR	Quadrennial Defense Review
SBS	British Special Boat Service

SF   Special Forces

SOCCENT   Special Operations Command Central

SOCOM   Special Operations Command

SOF   special operations forces

SOFLAM   Special Operations Forces Laser Acquisition Marker

UAV   unmanned aerial vehicle

UN   United Nations

USASOC   U.S. Army Special Operations Command

WMDs   weapons of mass destruction

I

THE LION'S DEN

March 1979 to September 10, 2001

*Whoever wishes to hear the clash of swords, let him come to
Maasada [the Lion's Den], where he will find courageous men
ready to die for the sake of God.*

—HASSAN IBN THABIT,
SEVENTH-CENTURY ARABIAN POET[1]

The revolt of Herat in March 1979 launched Afghanistan from a
sleepy tourist destination to the ultimate battleground of the Cold
War. What emerged from this event would bring Osama bin Laden
to Afghanistan five years later. In the wake of the Islamic Revolution in Iran,
revolutionary fervor quickly spread eastward to Afghanistan. And just as it had
been during the time of the Silk Road, the city of Herat was the thoroughfare.
Led by a local Afghan Army captain named Ismail Khan, a group of religious
Heratis set in motion a violent uprising against the communist Afghan regime.
Within days, the heads of over a dozen Soviet political advisors and their families stood on pikes throughout Herat's streets. And "as Herat burned, KGB
officers seethed."[2]

Under the rising sun on December 25, 1979, Soviet forces crossed the
Amu Darya River and entered the northern edge of Afghanistan. Two days
later, KGB paramilitary officers in Kabul stormed the Presidential Palace and
assassinated Afghan president Hafizullah Amin. It was the start of a new front
in the proxy war between the United States and the Soviet Union that would
have vast implications for Afghanistan over the next four decades.[3]

1

In the weeks after the first Soviet troops entered Afghanistan, the U.S. government formulated a covert strategy for this newfound front in the Cold War. National Security Advisor Zbigniew Brzezinski determined that "our ultimate goal is the withdrawal of Soviet troops from Afghanistan. . . . Even if this is not attainable, we should make the Soviet involvement as costly as possible."[4]

The emerging U.S. policy to respond to the Soviet invasion of Afghanistan sought to sponsor the Afghan mujahideen, or holy warriors, in their war to expel the Soviet invaders. The mujahideen were a conglomerate of Afghan rebels whose underlying solidarity stemmed from their Islamic beliefs. Some were Islamic fundamentalists; others were simply pious Muslims with a disdain for communist rule. By 1981, with CIA backing and weapons, "the rebels roamed freely in nearly all of Afghanistan's twenty-nine provinces."[5]

Nonetheless, the CIA's influence was limited due to its lack of physical access and relationships with the centers of power of the Afghan jihad. The CIA therefore turned to Pakistan and its Inter-Services Intelligence (ISI) for assistance. Pakistan saw the jihad, or holy war, as a monumental opportunity to exert influence on its neighbor to the west. Pakistani president Mohammad Zia-ul-Haq worried that a communist Afghan government could incite a Pashtun independence movement, an occurrence Zia feared would tear apart Pakistan. Zia was equally concerned that Pakistan would be surrounded by hostile neighbors, with the communist-leaning governments of Afghanistan to the west, India to the east, and the Soviet Union and China to the north. Zia sought complete political control of the war effort in order to establish a strategic proxy in Afghanistan, while the Americans simply wanted to attrite and expel the Soviets. Both the Americans and the Pakistanis knew that success in Afghanistan depended on each other's support.[6] By 1983 the triad of the covert war against the Soviets in Afghanistan—CIA-supplied weapons and money, ISI distribution and command, and Afghan mujahideen fighters—was in full force.

The small town of Jaji lies in the middle of the Hindu Kush mountain range along the eastern edge of Afghanistan. Less than ten miles away, the Durand Line marks the arbitrary border separating Pakistan and Afghanistan and serves as a constant reminder of British imperialism. Jaji sits at the tip of a small piece of Pakistani territory that juts sixty miles westward into Afghanistan like a parrot's

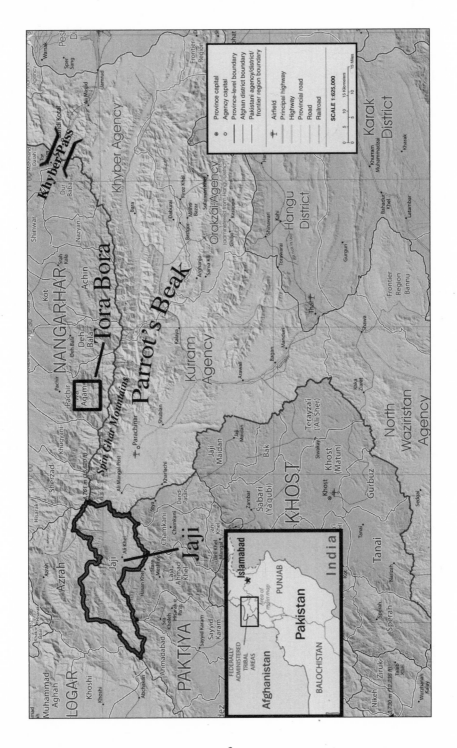

beak. The Spin Ghar mountain range, containing the six-mile sierra of Tora Bora, extends across the top of the beak. At the northern base of the protrusion lies the historic Khyber Pass, a break in the mountains crossed by Alexander the Great during his conquest of India.

In 1984, almost five years after the Soviet invasion of Afghanistan, Osama bin Laden reluctantly traveled to Jaji to observe the holy war. The son of one of the wealthiest Saudi families, bin Laden was a shy, devout Muslim and a financier of the Afghan jihad; he was not a warrior.[7] Despite his financial and logistical support for the Afghan mujahideen, bin Laden's fear of the battle-field had previously kept him out of Afghanistan. But during the month of Ramadan in 1984, he ventured across the Durand Line to visit an Afghan encampment at Jaji. One morning bin Laden awoke to Soviet bombardments that literally shook the mountains. After his hosts took positions to engage, bin Laden witnessed the mujahideen destroy four Soviet aircraft. Inspired by this experience, he promptly returned to Saudi Arabia and raised between $5 million and $10 million for the Afghan cause by the end of Ramadan.[8]

Bin Laden returned to Jaji two years later, this time the commander of a group of sixty Arab fighters. Bin Laden's first encounter with jihad had influenced him profoundly. The writings of Abdullah Azzam that spoke of every Muslim's duty to repel infidel invaders motivated bin Laden to take an increasingly important role in chauffeuring Arabs to the Afghan jihad. By the end of 1986, bin Laden, who now referred to himself as the Lion, had established the first all-Arab base in Afghanistan. Arrogantly located in the side of a mountain only three kilometers from a Soviet base, the Arabs at Maasada—the Lion's Den—lived an ascetic lifestyle. By early 1987, months of Soviet bombardments effectively isolated the cave dwelling bored into the mountains that separated Pakistan from Afghanistan.[9]

The holy month of Ramadan in the summer of 1987 defined the early bin Laden. Barely able to walk twenty meters at a time due to an illness, bin Laden had initiated a hasty retreat from Maasada after the deaths of two Arab fighters. Their overall Afghan commander, unimpressed by Arabs' tepidness, ordered their immediate return to the treacherous Lion's Den. During the twenty-two-day battle that ensued, bin Laden and his Arab fighters outflanked and repelled two hundred Spetsnaz commandos and destroyed a Soviet MiG, resulting in a Soviet retreat. The Battle of Jaji propelled Osama bin Laden from an unknown name to a war hero of the Afghan jihad, despite the minor battle's irrelevance to the overall war. In the Quran, the twenty-seventh night of Ramadan—known as Leilat al-Qadr—is the day when destiny is decided. For bin Laden on that day in 1987, the Quranic text was prophetic: "Leilat al Qadr is better than a thousand months."[10]

——— ✦◆✦ ———

Bloodied and bruised, the last Soviet troops crossed the Amu Darya River and left Afghanistan on February 15, 1989. The U.S. covert war had exceeded expectations: not only was the Soviet Union weakened and expelled, it was falling apart at its very core. The late Pakistani president Zia's vision for the covert war was also fulfilled. Pakistan now faced a crumbling empire to its north along with a weak government and strong proxy force in Afghanistan. However, according to author Steve Coll, "outside the Pakistan army itself, less than ten years after the Soviet invasion of Afghanistan, ISI had been transformed by CIA and Saudi subsidies into Pakistan's most powerful institution. Whatever unfolded now would require ISI's consent."[11]

The Soviets left Afghanistan in a state of conflict and chaos, fragmented by political, religious, and ethnic divisions. The weak communist regime led by Mohammad Najibullah remained in Kabul after the Soviet withdrawal but was doomed to collapse. The strongest military and political forces in Afghanistan were ISI-backed fundamentalists with little allegiance to the United States. Indeed, during the latter half of the 1980s, ISI sponsorship of Afghan mujahideen factions largely correlated to the degree of Islamist radicalism. On the other hand, the Tajiks, Uzbeks, and Hazaras represented a formidable fighting force in northern Afghanistan but lacked the backing of the ISI.[12] It was a recipe for a power vacuum, one that would be exploited by the Taliban and al Qaeda in the years to come. In the meantime, the war continued.

In early 1992 Ahmad Shah Massoud, a leader of the Tajik, Uzbek, and Hazara mujahideen, preempted a move by the ISI-sponsored radical Gulbuddin Hekmatyar and took control of Kabul, officially toppling the Najibullah government.[13] But while the ISI continued to support Hekmatyar, the United States largely withdrew from the region. A civil war ensued between Massoud, Hekmatyar, and a variety of smaller forces. By 1994 the fragmentation of Afghanistan that had started with the departure of Soviet forces was complete.[14]

Just as Afghanistan reached the pinnacle of strife and disintegration, a new force emerged from the chaos to impose order and stringent Islamic law, or sharia, on Afghanistan. This movement was composed mostly of students, or *talibs*, who had studied in religious schools along the Afghan-Pakistani border. Between the Afghans who had fought against the Soviets and those who had fled to refugee camps in Pakistan, the inaugural members of the Taliban were both militaristic and deeply religious. Indeed, these characteristics ensured that the Taliban had strong ties with the ISI from its inception. Led by Mullah Mohammed Omar, a Kandahari Pashtun of whom little is known, the Taliban's meteoric rise to power defied the very nature of the seemingly uncontrollable situation in Afghanistan.[15]

On November 3, 1994, a contingent of Taliban forces attacked the southern Afghan city of Kandahar. The local resistance gave way after two days of fighting, likely due to ISI influence and bribery. The Taliban captured old Soviet tanks, MiG-21 fighter planes, transport helicopters, and other remnants of the Soviet war. They also incorporated 2,500 men from a local militia into their ranks. In a matter of days, the Taliban had conquered Afghanistan's second largest city, enlisted several thousand troops, and commandeered advanced military technologies while only losing a dozen soldiers.[16]

The pace of the Taliban's ascent to power was stunning. By December 1994—just one month after the fall of Kandahar—the Taliban had gained over twelve thousand members. Two months later they controlled twelve of the thirty-one provinces in Afghanistan. By September 1995 the Taliban controlled the entire western portion of Afghanistan, including Herat. In the areas under its control, the Taliban implemented what journalist Ahmed Rashid called "the strictest interpretation of Sharia law ever seen in the Muslim world."[17] However, the Taliban also opened many of the country's roads in order to lower food prices and encourage commerce, disarmed militias, and imposed order after two decades of chaos. To the ethnic Pashtuns in southern Afghanistan, the Taliban represented an alternative to the Tajik- and Uzbek-dominated forces of northern Afghanistan.[18] The Taliban were ruthless, brutal, and oppressive; they were also the first political force in two decades to bring some semblance of stability to the lawless and war-torn country.

On September 26, 1996, columns of Taliban forces approached Kabul from four sides. Massoud withdrew his troops from the capital, knowing that even if he could repel the initial invasion, the bloody nature of the battle could undermine his public support. That night, a five-man team of Taliban operatives stormed the UN compound housing former president Najibullah, the communist president of Afghanistan from 1986 to 1992, and proceeded to beat, mutilate, kill, and hang Najibullah and his brother from a traffic post outside the Presidential Palace.[19] Najibullah's execution was a harbinger of the brutality to come:

> Within 24 hours of taking Kabul, the Taliban imposed the strictest Islamic system in place anywhere in the world. All women were banned from work, even though one quarter of Kabul's civil service, the entire elementary educational system and much of the health system were run by women. Girls' schools and colleges were closed down affecting more than 70,000 female students and a strict dress code of head-to-toe veils for women was imposed. There were fears that 25,000 families which were headed by war widows and depended on working and UN handouts would starve. Every day brought fresh pronouncements. "Thieves will have their hands and feet amputated, adulterers will be stoned to death and those taking liquor will be lashed," said an announcement on Radio Kabul on 28 September 1996.
>
> TV, videos, satellite dishes, music and all games including chess, football, and kite-flying were banned. . . . Taliban soldiers stood on main streets arresting men without beards. . . . As the newly formed Taliban religious police went about their business of enforcing "Sharia", Kabul was treated as an occupied city.[20]

By 1998 the Taliban had consolidated power, and only a small portion of northern Afghanistan lay outside their control. Ahmad Shah Massoud commanded the last force preventing a complete Taliban takeover. The ISI was partially responsible for the Taliban's rapid rise to power. Pakistan's powerful intelligence agency provided them with money, guidance, training camps, weapons, communication systems, and free movement across the border. While the Taliban often acted outside of ISI control and guidance, the relationship between the two endured.[21] Ultimately, as then Pakistani prime minister Benazir Bhutto recalled, the Taliban were "given carte blanche."[22]

Osama bin Laden arrived in Afghanistan just before the fall of Kabul in mid-1996. In the aftermath of the Soviet withdrawal from Afghanistan in 1989, bin Laden returned to Saudi Arabia as a hero of the Afghan jihad. However, he remained deeply connected to his past activities in Afghanistan. Under the veil of secrecy, bin Laden consolidated his group of Arab militants from the Afghan jihad into an organization that would become al Qaeda. Using his newfound status and drawing upon his experiences commanding Arab militants in Afghanistan, bin Laden approached the Saudi royal family to offer his services for the next holy wars. First, bin Laden proposed waging jihad against the government of Yemen. Soon afterward, the Saudi government revoked bin Laden's passport to prevent foreign travel and discontinue his subversive activities in Yemen. When Saddam Hussein invaded Kuwait in August 1990, bin Laden once again approached the Saudi government. He argued that he could lead a successful jihad to expel the Iraqis just as he did with the Soviets in Afghanistan. He was snubbed in favor of American troops, half a million of whom arrived in Saudi Arabia and its neighbors in preparation for attacking Iraqi forces in Kuwait. Bin Laden was outraged. Instead of leading a holy war that he viewed an Islamic duty, American infidels now occupied the most sacred lands of Islam.[23]

Over the next four years bin Laden became increasingly disenchanted with the Saudi government. In 1992 the Sudanese government persuaded him to move to Sudan. According to author Lawrence Wright, bin Laden "was being offered an entire country in which to operate freely."[24] It was during his time in Sudan that bin Laden developed and cultivated al Qaeda's ideology and operational capacity. Among the operations to which al Qaeda was tangentially related were the 1993 World Trade Center bombing and the downing of U.S. helicopters in Mogadishu, Somalia. Bin Laden's actions attracted the attention of the Algerian, Yemeni, Egyptian, and Saudi governments, which saw him as instigating insurgencies in their countries. On March 5, 1994, at the behest of the Egyptian government, King Fahd of Saudi Arabia revoked bin Laden's citizenship. The Saudi interior ministry also forced the bin Laden family to sever its financial ties with Osama, including his monthly stipend and his $7 million stake in the family company.[25]

Bin Laden's business ventures in Sudan were failing as well. On May 18, 1996, under pressure from the United States due to his complicity in the attempted assassination of Egyptian president Hosni Mubarak as well as plans to bomb UN headquarters in New York, the Sudanese government expelled bin Laden. Estimates of bin Laden's financial losses in Sudan vary from $20 million to $160 million. Either way, bin Laden came to Sudan as a Saudi millionaire and left as a broke, citizenless miscreant. As the Sudanese government warned and the U.S. government passively endorsed, he then left for the most likely destination: Afghanistan.[26]

On May 18, 1996, bin Laden arrived in Jalalabad—just sixty miles northeast of Jaji—uninvited and without the consent of the Taliban.[27] Upon arrival he received support from local warlords Mohammad Younis Khalis, Gulbuddin Hekmatyar, and Abdurrab Rasul Sayyaf.[28] *The 9/11 Commission Report* noted that "Pakistani intelligence officers reportedly introduced bin Ladin to Taliban leaders in Kandahar . . . out of an apparent hope that he would now expand the [terrorist training] camps [near Khost] and make them available for training Kashmiri militants."[29] The Taliban were initially wary of bin Laden.[30] Bin Laden's ties were with the mujahideen in eastern Afghanistan, who remained at odds with the burgeoning Taliban movement. Little was known by the Taliban about bin Laden beyond his participation in the jihad against the Soviets. The Saudi government had also charged Mullah Omar with containing bin Laden. It remains unclear how bin Laden assuaged Taliban suspicions, although one account indicates that he had provided $3 million to fund the Taliban's conquest of Kabul.[31] Nonetheless, he succeeded in acquiring the Taliban's acceptance of his presence, marking the start of the most important symbiotic relationship in the history of both the Taliban and al Qaeda.

Bin Laden soon moved to Tora Bora. From his cave dwelling there, he issued his "Declaration of War against the Americans Occupying the Land of the Two Holy Places" on August 23, 1996.[32] The document is a surprisingly candid view into the ideology of bin Laden and al Qaeda. In this long, uncompromising diatribe, bin Laden weaves radical Islamic theology with a conspiratorial view of modern history into a foundational manifesto for al Qaeda. Nonetheless, it was a serious declaration of war:

> Those youths know that their rewards in fighting you, the USA, is double than their rewards in fighting some one else not from the people of the book. They have no intention except to enter paradise by killing you.

An infidel, and enemy of God like you, cannot be in the same hell with his righteous executioner.[33]

Bin Laden's presence in Afghanistan posed questions for the Taliban regime. Soon after bin Laden's declaration of war, Mullah Omar dispatched an envoy to meet with him. Bin Laden's declaration was neither quiet nor harmless, and it violated the promises that Mullah Omar had made to the Saudi royal family. Members of the Taliban leadership were divided in their opinion of bin Laden. There was much ideological agreement, and bin Laden was viewed as a significant source of financial support for the new regime (the Taliban did not know that he was, for the most part, broke). And yet bin Laden's insolence could exacerbate the Taliban's already shaky standing within the international community. In the end, the delegation offered to protect bin Laden as long as he did not attack Saudi Arabia or speak to the press. Bin Laden accepted, although his promise did not last long.[34]

In March 1997 CNN journalists Peter Bergen and Peter Arnett ventured to bin Laden's cave in Tora Bora for one of his only television interviews. Posing next to his Soviet AK-74, bin Laden explained his rationale for declaring war on the United States. When asked about his future plans at the conclusion of the interview, bin Laden responded with a sinister smirk, "You'll see them and hear about them in the media, God willing."[35]

Irritated by bin Laden's violation of their agreement, Mullah Omar summoned him to Kandahar for their first meeting. Under the pretext of an uncovered kidnapping plot, Omar instructed bin Laden to move to Kandahar so that the Taliban could better protect him and monitor his actions. As Wright details in his book, "Omar personally extended his protection to bin Laden, but he said that all interviews must come to a stop."[36] Bin Laden and his family moved into a dilapidated compound in the Taliban capital three days later.[37]

Al Qaeda gradually regrouped in Afghanistan. Ayman al-Zawahiri joined bin Laden in Kandahar in May 1997. Zawahiri—who would become al Qaeda's second-in-command—was the leader of the Egyptian Islamic Jihad, a terrorist organization focused on overthrowing Hosni Mubarak's secular Egyptian government. An assortment of other militants joined bin Laden at the Tarnak Farms compound near Kandahar, including many who had fought alongside him in Afghanistan in the 1980s. In January 1998 Zawahiri drafted a document intended to unite the disparate jihadist groups in the region. On February 23, 1998, the International Islamic Front for Jihad against Jews and Crusaders issued Zawahiri's proclamation. It was signed by the who's-who of Islamist terrorism, including bin Laden, Zawahiri, and leaders from Pakistani and Bangladeshi terrorist groups.[38] Thus, terrorist organizations that used to be motivated by domestic and regional issues suddenly united and shifted their stated focus to the United States. The directive at the end of the document highlights its significance:

> The ruling to kill the Americans and their allies—civilians and military— is an individual duty for every Muslim who can do it in any country in which it is possible to do it, in order to liberate the al-Aqsa Mosque [in Jerusalem] and the holy mosque [in Mecca] from their grip, and in order for their armies to move out of all the 2 lands of Islam [Saudi Arabia], defeated and unable to threaten any Muslim. This is in accordance with the words of Almighty God, "and fight the pagans all together as they fight you all together," and "fight them until there is no more tumult or oppression, and there prevail justice and faith in God."[39]

The proclamation to kill Americans anywhere marked a turning point for al Qaeda. Islamic militants worldwide flocked to the ISI-subsidized training camps that al Qaeda ran in Afghanistan. Bin Laden held press conferences with regional and international media outlets, infuriating Mullah Omar. Money began to flow into al Qaeda's coffers. However, some in the conglomerate of signatories to the proclamation resented the shift in focus. Their fight was against their own oppressive governments, which they viewed as the "near enemy," and America represented a distraction. Some organizations embraced the shift, causing individual militants to leave out of principle; other organizations adopted the rhetoric but disregarded its implementation. Nonetheless, al Qaeda now had the resources necessary to begin enacting its ideology.[40]

The 1996 declaration of war and the 1998 proclamation to kill Americans worldwide also attracted attention within the U.S. government. At the start of 1996, the CIA had set up a unit, code-named Alec Station, dedicated to tracking Osama bin Laden. Led by veteran CIA analyst Michael Scheuer, Alec Station was an experimental fusion cell that centralized all elements of intelligence pertaining to bin Laden. The CIA chose to focus on bin Laden because of his rising significance in the world of international terrorism.[41] By mid-1998 the Agency had a notable intelligence collection campaign directed toward bin Laden. It also began planning a variety of clandestine operations aimed at neutralizing him, albeit initially without the use of lethal force. As a result of the intelligence community's efforts, an obscured and incomplete—but nonetheless disconcerting—picture of al Qaeda and bin Laden emerged.[42]

The creation of the CIA's bin Laden unit was a prescient and astute—if not fortuitous—move. In the years since the end of the Soviet jihad, bin Laden had turned a small group of disheveled Arab fighters into a global terrorist network that would execute the deadliest foreign attack on American soil in history. Under bin Laden's leadership, al Qaeda had become a lethal and subversive organization determined to pursue its radical Islamist agenda through the use of force. As al Qaeda's actions would soon show, this organization was unlike other terrorist entities and merited the attention it received.

On August 7, 1998, exactly eight years after the arrival of U.S. troops in Saudi Arabia for the Gulf War, members of al Qaeda drove trucks brimming with explosives into the U.S. embassies in Kenya and Tanzania. The attacks killed 224 people and injured over 4,500, mostly Kenyans and Tanzanians. While some within Alec Station were convinced before the attacks that bin Laden intended to attack U.S. targets and had advocated a more aggressive approach toward stopping him, no one in the U.S. intelligence community had provided a specific warning about the attack. As a whole, the U.S. government did not take bin Laden seriously. Even when an Egyptian member of al Qaeda entered the U.S. Embassy in Nairobi and warned the CIA about the impending attack, it was dismissed as unreliable intelligence.[43] Until this point, Osama bin Laden and al Qaeda had been only tangentially associated with terrorist attacks. But the U.S. embassy bombings in East Africa left no room for interpretation or error: al Qaeda was determined to strike the United States and its interests.[44]

The Clinton administration responded by launching seventy-five cruise missiles to the surmised location of bin Laden and some terrorist training camps in Afghanistan, as well as thirteen cruise missiles to destroy a chemical factory in Sudan suspected of making weapons of mass destruction (WMDs). The strike in Afghanistan missed bin Laden by a few hours, and intelligence later determined that the destroyed chemical plant was one of Sudan's only pharmaceutical factories. Some evidence exists that the ISI had warned the Taliban of the impending attack, who in turn informed Osama bin Laden to ensure his survival.[45] While the Afghan cruise missile strike missed its intended target, it succeeded in killing a team of ISI operatives at a camp that bin Laden intended to visit.[46] A DIA intelligence assessment reflected the U.S. concerns that emerged from the strike:

> Bin Laden's al Qaeda network was able to expand under the safe sanctuary extended by the Taliban following Pakistan directives. If there is any doubt on that issue, consider the location of bin Laden's camp targeted by U.S. cruise missiles. . . . Positioned on the border between Afghanistan and Pakistan it was built by Pakistani contractors, and funded by the Pakistan Inter-Services Intelligence Directorate. . . . The real host in that facility was the Pakistani ISI. If this was later to become bin Laden's base, then serious questions are raised by the early relationship between bin Laden and ISI.[47]

Richard Clarke, the chair of the Counterterrorism Support Group on the National Security Council at the time of the cruise missile strikes, went further than the DIA assessment:

> I believed that if Pakistan's ISID [Inter-Services Intelligence Directorate] wanted to capture bin Laden or tell us where he was, they could have done so with little effort. They did not cooperate with us because ISID saw al Qaeda as helpful to the Taliban.[48]

The U.S. embassy bombings and their aftermath changed the nature of the situation both for al Qaeda and the United States. The cruise missile strikes cemented bin Laden's reputation as a stalwart champion of anti-Americanism and overshadowed his callous brutality. The U.S government now considered bin Laden to be a modest but serious threat, and President Clinton authorized the CIA to use lethal force against him. The intelligence and law enforcement efforts that followed the bombings revealed the global, subversive, and lethal nature of al Qaeda. But while the mentality of the U.S. government—especially the CIA—shifted, the resources behind those efforts stagnated.[49]

The bombings also changed the relationship between Osama bin Laden and Mullah Omar, and likewise between al Qaeda and the Taliban. Mullah Omar angrily summoned bin Laden in the aftermath of the U.S. embassy bombings. Osama apologized, offered to leave Afghanistan, and, in a rare show of submission, swore allegiance to Omar. He referred to Omar as the "noble emir" and commander of the faithful, terms used in the distant past to refer to the caliph of the Muslim world. In a marked shift in dynamics, a friendship emerged between bin Laden and Omar. From this point forth, Mullah Omar wholeheartedly protected bin Laden. Indeed, when Saudi prince Turki al-Faisal and ISI director Naseem Rana next met with Mullah Omar about the previously agreed-upon extradition of bin Laden to Saudi Arabia, Omar changed his mind, refused, and proceeded to furiously insult the Saudi prince. Mullah Omar risked losing one of his two lone international patrons simply to defend bin Laden.[50]

The cooperation between the Taliban, al Qaeda, and Pakistan's ISI reached new levels over the next two years. Al Qaeda gained complete operational control of the terrorist camps in Afghanistan. While the ISI provided financial and logistical support for these training centers, the Taliban gave bin Laden free rein. An estimated thirty thousand militants from around the world were trained in the camps run by al Qaeda between 1996 and 2001.[51] On the battlefield in Afghanistan, these three organizations acted in unison. Ahmed Rashid writes that more than five thousand of the Taliban's fifteen thousand troops at the September 2000 battle for Taloqan were not from Afghanistan. Of those five thousand foreign militants, there were nearly three thousand Pakistanis, one thousand from the Islamic Movement of Uzbekistan (IMU), and hundreds of fighters from Chechnya, Kashmir, China, the Philippines, and Arab nations. Furthermore, the ISI was supporting the Taliban operation at every level. In addition to supplying the Taliban with one hundred troops from the Pakistani Frontier Corps to coordinate communications and artillery barrages at Taloqan, "Pakistani officers were directing the Taliban campaign in league with al Qaeda and the Taliban."[52] According to American intelligence reports, ISI colonels regularly met with bin Laden and members of al Qaeda to synchronize the flow of militants to and from the training camps. It is important to note that while the ISI used its relationship with the Taliban and al Qaeda to advance its regional interests in Afghanistan and Kashmir, there is no evidence to show that the ISI collaborated with al Qaeda on its international terrorist attacks on the United States.[53] Nonetheless, Afghanistan had become the indisputable worldwide leader in training terrorists and the epicenter of Islamist terrorism.

On October 12, 2000, three al Qaeda operatives steered a small boat laden with explosives next to the USS *Cole*, a billion-dollar Navy destroyer refueling in Yemen. The al Qaeda operatives detonated the explosives upon reaching the center of the warship's port side, blowing a forty-foot hole in the ship and killing seventeen American sailors. In preparation for the American response, bin Laden dispersed the core al Qaeda leadership among major Afghan cities to protect his chain of command. But no military response came. Although the attack generated substantial concern in the intelligence community, the top civilian and military leadership precluded direct action for political reasons. Between the failure of the cruise missile strikes after the U.S. embassy bombings, President Clinton's pernicious impeachment process, the timing of the attack at the end of his presidency, and the failure to clearly attribute the attack to al Qaeda at the time, military retaliation was not viewed as a feasible option.[54]

The USS *Cole* bombing did, however, accelerate the isolation of the Taliban from the international community and further exposed the al Qaeda–Taliban–ISI triad. On December 19, 2000, the United Nations passed a resolution aimed at the Taliban, al Qaeda, and implicitly Pakistan. Resolution 1333 demanded that the Taliban close all terrorist training camps, turn over Osama bin Laden, and halt illegal drug activities regarding the opium and heroin trade. The resolution also imposed an arms embargo, froze al Qaeda's financial assets, and called on all member nations to refrain from supporting the Taliban. Although the resolution did not explicitly identify Pakistan, the international directive was clearly designed to ban almost every aspect of the Taliban-Pakistani relationship.[55] The UN resolution represented an important but insufficient step in combating al Qaeda. The Taliban, al Qaeda, and Pakistan's ISI did not adhere to any aspect of international law. And since only three countries—Pakistan, Saudi Arabia, and the United Arab Emirates—officially recognized the Taliban as the legitimate government of Afghanistan, the tangible outcomes of the UN resolution were minimal.

President George W. Bush brought little change to U.S. policy on al Qaeda during his first eight months in office. The newly inaugurated administration largely disregarded—and at the very least underestimated—the threat that al Qaeda posed. However, the U.S. intelligence community was convinced that an attack was imminent. George Tenet, the director of the CIA, said that the situation could not "get any worse" and the "system was blinking red."[56] Between electronic intercepts, human assets, and the disappearance of key al Qaeda operatives, all indications pointed to an impending attack.[57] On August 6, 2001, the headline of the "President's Daily Brief," a daily CIA compilation of the most sensitive and pertinent intelligence for the president, was "Bin Laden Determined to Strike in U.S."[58] But while American intelligence and law enforcement discovered fragments of al Qaeda's next plot, no specific and actionable threat assessment ever emerged.[59] At all levels of government and society, the United States of America was woefully unready for the events of September 11, 2001.

2

SCRAMBLING TO RESPOND

September 11 to September 18, 2001

Every day since has been September 12.

— CONDOLEEZZA RICE[1]

On the morning of September 11, 2001, America was under attack. Nineteen al Qaeda operatives hijacked four domestic flights bound for California. At 8:46 a.m., American Airlines flight 11 crashed into the north tower of the World Trade Center in New York City. Seventeen minutes later, United Airlines flight 175 hit the south tower. At 9:37 a.m., American Airlines flight 77 hit the western wall of the Pentagon. At 10:03 a.m., United Airlines flight 93 crashed in an open field in rural Pennsylvania. By 10:30 a.m., both towers of the World Trade Center had collapsed. Across the Eastern Seaboard, 103 minutes left 2,973 people dead.[2]

President George W. Bush was in Sarasota, Florida, to promote education reform when the first plane struck the World Trade Center. To most of the world, including the president, news of the first collision suggested an accident or isolated incident. When the second plane hit, perceptions of coincidence rapidly gave way to recognition of an attack. Andrew Card, the president's chief of staff, interrupted the president as he read to a group of second graders and whispered, "A second plane hit the second tower. America is under attack." Within an hour the president boarded Air Force One for a series of secret movements designed to protect America's most important leader.[3]

In the Pentagon, Secretary of Defense Donald Rumsfeld was meeting with members of Congress to discuss his vision for military transformation when the attacks began. Every four years, the Department of Defense (DOD) conducts the Quadrennial Defense Review (QDR) under congressional mandate as a strategic reassessment of threats, priorities, and challenges to American defense and security. The 2001 QDR reflected Rumsfeld's effort of "transforming America's defense for the 21st century."[4] His vision for the armed services was a nimble, high-tech, surgical organization capable of "projecting and sustaining US forces in distant anti-access environments" and "decisively defeating any adversary."[5] Despite the attacks on the twin towers, Rumsfeld refrained from moving to the protected National Military Command Center (NMCC) because of an intelligence briefing scheduled for 9:30 a.m. in his office. The Pentagon shook when American Airlines flight 77 hit, and Rumsfeld impulsively rushed to assist the first responders. He then entered the NMCC and raised the military alert level to Defense Condition 3 (DefCon 3) to increase U.S. force readiness around the world. The president had authorized the Air Force to shoot down any hijacked aircraft, and Rumsfeld worked vigorously to clarify and tighten the rules of engagement.[6]

CIA Director George Tenet was eating breakfast with former senator David Boren when the chief of his security detail alerted him to the first attack. Unlike the president, Tenet instantly attributed the attack to al Qaeda and returned to headquarters at Langley, Virginia, where he met with the top CIA leadership. The subsequent evacuation of CIA headquarters left only a few Counterterrorism Center (CTC) officials with the resources to investigate the crisis. But by midday, intelligence analysts had connected two of the hijackers to al Qaeda.[7]

On the morning of September 11, Secretary of State Colin Powell was in Lima, Peru, for a meeting of the Organization of American States. News of the first plane hitting the north tower reached the general-turned-diplomat during a breakfast with Peruvian president Alejandro Toledo. When the second plane hit the south tower, Powell immediately suspected Osama bin Laden. In a display of composure, Powell finished a series of meetings and then boarded his airplane to return to the American capital.[8]

Osama bin Laden and his deputy Ayman al-Zawahiri were twelve miles west of Jaji in the Afghan town of Khost when the hijacked planes hit their intended targets.[9] Anticipating American retaliation, Bin Laden dispersed al Qaeda's leadership across Afghanistan. He also had orchestrated a targeted assassination that decapitated the only serious military force opposing the Taliban in Afghanistan. On September 9, two days before the terrorist attacks on the United States, two al Qaeda operatives posing as reporters detonated a suicide bomb concealed in a video camera and killed Ahmad Shah Massoud, the leader of the Northern Alliance.[10]

Massoud had played an important role in Afghanistan's history up until his untimely assassination two days before the September 11 terrorist attacks. An ethnic Tajik born in the Panjshir Valley of northeastern Afghanistan, Massoud spent the majority of his life fighting. During the Soviet occupation of Afghanistan, Massoud gained national renown for his effective command of a couple thousand mujahideen. By 1982 Massoud and his forces had repelled six Soviet offensives, earning him the nickname "the Lion of the Panjshir." Unlike more radical factions in Afghanistan that relied upon ISI sponsorship, Massoud depended almost entirely on popular support. In fact, it was not until the mid-1980s, when the United States sought to develop relationships independent of Pakistan's ISI, that Massoud began receiving significant external support.[11]

Massoud emerged on top from the three years of conflict that followed the Soviet withdrawal. In mid-1992, his forces took control of Kabul. Even still, the conflict continued between Massoud and his archrival, the ISI-backed Gulbuddin Hekmatyar.[12] Massoud could never escape his ethnicity; even as an inclusive and charismatic leader, he was viewed by Afghanistan's Pashtun plurality as first and foremost a Tajik partisan. Both Hekmatyar and later the Taliban exploited these ethnic divisions and incited Pashtun unity to undermine Massoud. By 1998, two years after the Taliban's rapid rise to power across Afghanistan, Massoud was the lone impediment to complete Taliban control.

Massoud was the glue that held together the anti-Taliban resistance in Afghanistan. He commanded the Northern Alliance, a conglomerate of ethnic Tajiks, Uzbeks, Hazaras, and certain Pashtun factions that represented the sole organized opposition to the Taliban regime. By late 2001, Massoud's Northern Alliance only controlled the northeastern corner of Afghanistan and a pocket of resistance near Mazar-i-Sharif. Nonetheless, the Northern Alliance had years of experience fighting the Taliban and remained a powerful and popular force in northern Afghanistan. Massoud's assassination dealt a devastating blow to what would become America's biggest ally in the country at a strategically critical juncture.

The president addressed the nation from the safety of the White House bunker on the evening of September 11. In a remark directed toward the Taliban, he avowed, "We will make no distinction between the terrorists who committed these acts and those who harbor them."[13] The Taliban had unwittingly tied its destiny to the future of al Qaeda, and the president's speech determined the immediate fate of both.

In the aftermath of the attacks, each agency in the national security apparatus scrambled to understand and retaliate against al Qaeda. The natural place for the president to turn in a time of war and unprecedented attack was the Department of Defense. But to the dismay of the cabinet, the DOD did not maintain an off-the-shelf operations plan (OPLAN) for Afghanistan. Although the military constantly prepared and refined OPLANs for hundreds of scenarios, the only relevant resource was a list of some static Taliban and al Qaeda targets that excluded any plan for inserting ground troops.[14] Just six months before, Rumsfeld had told Gen. Richard Myers, then vice chairman of the Joint Chiefs of Staff (JCS), "we have an opportunity [for military transformation] that we must not squander . . . [because] the country faced no major strategic challenge abroad." On the other hand, Rumsfeld warned that the "most reckless course of action would be to dwell on old threats."[15] In hindsight, Rumsfeld's judgments appeared both contradictory and prescient. And at a defining moment for DOD, it was empty-handed.

By contrast, the CIA maintained extensive knowledge on Afghanistan and al Qaeda as a result of its role in expelling the Soviets one decade earlier. Even though CIA operations in Afghanistan had declined rapidly after the Soviets withdrew in 1989, the relationships between Afghan leaders and the Agency remained. Michael Scheuer, the head of the CIA's bin Laden unit from 1996 to 1999, stated that "in the south, in [the Taliban capital of] Kandahar, we had a long-term association with some of those [Afghan] tribal leaders. By '96, we had been involved with some of them for 15 years."[16] In fact, the CIA had established over one hundred sources, subsources, and relationships across eight tribal networks in Afghanistan by September 11.[17] Despite the lack of personnel on the ground in Afghanistan on September 11 and the CIA's failure to anticipate the specific attack, the Agency possessed the relationships, experience, and understanding of al Qaeda and Afghanistan to respond.[18]

After September 11, National Security Council (NSC) meetings became the mechanism for the Bush administration to decide on the political objectives to be obtained through the use of force, also known as policy, and coordinate them across the various government agencies in the national security apparatus. President Bush officially chaired these cabinet-level meetings composed of his principal advisors, or war cabinet, although responsibility for most of the coordination fell to National Security Advisor Condoleezza Rice. While the vice president, secretary of defense, and secretary of state constitute the only statutory members of the NSC, nonstatutory members of the cabinet and their deputies often attended. The NSC generally shared responsibility with the Department of Defense in formulating strategy, or the way in which the United States employed force to achieve its policy. Operations—the individual military engagements—and the specific tactics used in an operation were primarily the domain of the Defense Department. Nevertheless, as the primary forum for the president to manage the war, NSC meetings did when appropriate address issues of operations and tactics. These bureaucratic processes and institutional responsibilities provided the contours for the development of a U.S. response to the September 11 terrorist attacks.

The NSC meeting on the morning of September 13 sought to define the scope of the impending war. National Security Advisor Rice began the meeting by briefing the NSC on three basic options. The first identified al Qaeda as the only enemy, under the assumption that the Taliban would yield to U.S. demands. The second assumed that the Taliban would be uncooperative and placed both al Qaeda and the Taliban in American crosshairs. The third option focused on a broad campaign against terrorism worldwide, including operations to "eliminate the Iraq threat."[19] Disagreement arose over which option to choose. The debate that ensued largely focused on whether to limit the war to the Taliban and al Qaeda in Afghanistan or to engage in a broader "global war on terrorism." Richard Armitage, the deputy secretary of state, favored the second option so as to shock and disrupt the worldwide network of terrorists headquartered in Afghanistan. However, Defense Secretary Donald Rumsfeld, his deputy Paul Wolfowitz, and Under Secretary of Defense for Policy Douglas Feith supported the broader third option. According to Feith, "Wolfowitz warned against focusing narrowly on al Qaida in Afghanistan."[20] And in a meeting with the top defense and military officials the next day, Rumsfeld

21

instructed them, "Don't over-elevate the importance of al Qaida."[21] In his memoir, Feith summed up the position by stating, "As we saw it, 9/11 did not mean simply that the United States had an al Qaida problem. We had a terrorism problem. A strategic response to 9/11 would have to take account of the threat from other terrorist groups."[22] Feith later explained his view of the interagency debate in more detail:

> The CIA and State Department sometimes operated on the basis of narrow considerations that ignored important strategic objectives. . . . Once the president decided that our first majority military action would be in Afghanistan, a debate arose on what to target there. CIA and State Department officials wanted to target al Qaeda only and not the Taliban. CIA officials argued forcefully that we should not make an enemy of the Taliban. According to that perspective, if we attack the Taliban, we would be driving Pashtuns into the Taliban's arms and laying the groundwork for a north-south civil war in Afghanistan. When we in the Pentagon heard that argument—we thought that the CIA folks were missing the strategic point that the United States had an interest in hitting the Taliban, as a state supporter of terrorism, so hard that it would become a lesson for all other state supporters. If we hit only al Qaeda targets and spared the Taliban, we would not be sending the necessary signal to other state supporters. We focused on state supporters because they were a visible part of the global terrorist network and we could pressure them to pull in the reins on the terrorist operatives, who were by and large not visible to our intelligence community. So if we wanted to have an effect on the terrorist operatives in hiding, we had to affect the policies and behavior of the state supporters.[23]

Deputy Director of the CIA John McLaughlin disagreed with Feith's assertion that the CIA advocated against targeting the Taliban:

> I respect Doug Feith but disagree with him on this issue. The whole point was to ally ourselves with the Northern Alliance in order to defeat the Taliban. What else do you call the Taliban in those circumstances other than an enemy?[24]

Nevertheless, the CIA displayed its dominance on the issues of Afghanistan and al Qaeda during the September 13 NSC meeting. Tenet brought along the energetic and animated chief of CTC Cofer Black to sell their proposal. The CIA had put together an integrated plan for covert action to retaliate against al Qaeda and the Taliban. Based on an experimental force structure, CIA paramilitary teams would insert with special operations teams to direct close air support and act as a force multiplier for indigenous Afghan factions. Black staged a dramatic performance and claimed, "When we are through with them, they will have flies walking across their eyeballs."[25] The president asked how long it would take to defeat the Taliban and al Qaeda once the joint teams deployed, and Black responded, "A matter of weeks."[26] Neither Tenet nor anyone else at the meeting concurred. Although the military did not present a concept of operations, the CIA's plan impressed the president.[27]

At the State Department, Secretary of State Colin Powell and his deputy Richard Armitage worked to develop a diplomatic strategy for the overall response. They immediately recognized Pakistan as the key to diplomatic efforts. Despite shaky U.S.-Pakistan relations, Powell and Armitage developed a list of seven demands for the Pakistani government, including stopping all al Qaeda operatives at the border, granting blanket overflight and landing rights, condemning the September 11 attacks, and breaking all support and diplomatic relations with the Taliban. Armitage met with Pakistani ambassador Maleeha Lodhi and Lt. Gen. Mahmud Ahmed, the pro-Taliban chief of Pakistan's Inter-Services Intelligence who happened to be in Washington, and issued the seven demands. For much of his career at the ISI, Ahmed led Pakistan's drive to develop the Taliban as Pakistan's strategic proxy in Afghanistan, and these seemingly outrageous demands undermined both his ideology and his previous efforts. Nonetheless, Lodhi and Ahmed passed the message to Gen. Pervez Musharraf, the president of Pakistan.[28]

President Musharraf had a long history of supporting Islamist militants and using insurgents as a tool of Pakistan's foreign policy and was not necessarily predisposed to side with the United States. Musharraf had risen through the ranks of the Pakistani Army and was appointed chief of army staff by then prime minister Nawaz Sharif in 1998 for his supposed loyalty to the civilian establishment and his lack of ethnic ties to the Punjabi officer corps. In the first half of 1999, General Musharraf masterminded a disastrous military operation in the Kargil district of Kashmir, possibly without the knowledge of Prime Minister Sharif. Pakistani soldiers and jihadists covertly crossed the Line of Control, the division between Pakistani and Indian forces, and took over Indian military positions. The limited war escalated drastically when Pakistani officials began hinting at the use of nuclear weapons if Indian forces entered Pakistan. Musharraf had adeptly forced Sharif into a corner: retreating would make Sharif look weak, while continuing the conflict was a path to full-scale war. In the end, Sharif flew to Washington and on July 4, 1999, and negotiated a unilateral cease-fire and withdrawal to behind the Line of Control. Three months later, Sharif attempted to remove his renegade chief of army staff while Musharraf was returning from a trip to Sri Lanka. In turn, Musharraf and his army colleagues orchestrated an impromptu coup d'état and arrested Sharif. General Musharraf proclaimed a state of emergency and declared himself chief executive of Pakistan in order to, in his words, "give it a civilian façade."[29]

Musharraf's audacity and adventurism would play an important role in the immediate aftermath of the September 11 terrorist attacks. Indeed, Musharraf contemplated whether to succumb to or confront the United States. After receiving the seven demands, he gathered his generals and "war-gamed the United States as an adversary."[30] The United States had forced Pakistan to pick sides, although it was unclear which side Musharraf would ultimately choose.

When Armitage called the Pakistani president on September 13, Musharraf agreed to all seven American demands, albeit with some reservations. Musharraf wanted to sever diplomatic relations with the Taliban immediately, but Armitage delayed this action so that they could attempt to persuade the Taliban to extradite bin Laden and secure two American hostages under Taliban control. At the next NSC meeting, Powell reported to the president the progress achieved outside of the interagency process. Rumsfeld, "clearly not happy" with the circumvention of this process, gruffly asked for a copy of the demands.[31] In a diplomatic coup indicative of the worldwide sympathy to the United States during the immediate aftermath of 9/11, Powell and Armitage had seemingly changed the dynamics of international relations in South and Central Asia in a matter of hours.[32]

On the surface, Pakistan's reversal was remarkable. The events of September 11 had occurred at the height of the relationship between the ISI, the Taliban, and al Qaeda. But two days later Pakistan renounced its twenty-year undertaking to cultivate a strategic proxy of Islamist militants in Afghanistan. Now Pakistan agreed to sever all relationships with the Taliban and al Qaeda and assist the United States in a military campaign against its former allies. CIA Director Tenet considered Pakistan's turnaround to be "the most important post-9/11 strategic development after the takedown of the Afghan sanctuary."[33] Pakistan promptly stopped its financial and logistical support of the Taliban, recalled its military advisors in Afghanistan, and began to cooperate with the United States on counterterrorism efforts aimed at al Qaeda. But while the overt forms of support quickly ended, Pakistan's ISI continued its relationship with the Taliban under the veil of secrecy.

Many within the Pakistani government disagreed with President Musharraf's decision to side with the Americans, and the deep-seated historical bond between the ISI and the Taliban proved too strong to be overcome in a matter of days. The Pakistanis understood the distinction between the Taliban and al Qaeda far better than the U.S. government at the time, and few Pakistani officials possessed qualms about applying different policies toward the two disparate organizations. Indeed, Musharraf faced ardent opposition when he convened the nine corps commanders—the men who held serious political power in Pakistan—to discuss the seven demands. But he was ultimately able to convince them to accept the U.S. demands in their entirety by arguing that India would fulfill whatever Pakistan refused. Nonetheless, Musharraf left the meeting knowing that he would have to replace a significant contingent of his top leadership because of their commitment to Islamic fundamentalism and the Taliban.[34]

A joint session of Congress met and passed the Authorization for the Use of Military Force on September 14, 2001. The one-page joint resolution authorized the president to use "all necessary and appropriate force against those nations, organizations, or persons he determines planned, authorized, committed, or aided the terrorist attacks that occurred on September 11, 2001, or harbored such organizations or persons." Congress provided the president with the broad but vague authority to use force to prevent "any future acts of international terrorism."[35]

The outlines of a broader national response to the terrorist attacks emerged at a retreat held by the president for his war cabinet at Camp David over the weekend of September 15–16. Tenet presented first. Along with Cofer Black, who so masterfully sold the initial concept to the president two days earlier, Tenet detailed how CIA operatives would deploy to Afghanistan and support Afghan tribes to "destroy al Qaeda and close the safe haven."[36] The CIA would clear the way for special operations units to attach to anti-Taliban military factions across the country. To hunt al Qaeda's leadership, Tenet suggested using the CIA's Predator unmanned aerial vehicles (UAVs) retrofitted with Hellfire antitank missiles. Tenet then described the CIA's plan for covert operations against al Qaeda across the world. To enact his ambitious agenda, he requested broad authority from the president to use lethal force, detain members of al Qaeda from around the world, initiate numerous clandestine activities and secret communications with rogue or unfriendly nations, and distribute large sums of money to advance U.S. interests. The CIA intended to bring the war to Afghanistan and attack al Qaeda across ninety-two countries.[37] Not only did the CIA describe such a comprehensive plan, but they could begin conducting these operations immediately.[38]

In contrast to the CIA's sweeping, global, covert war against America's new-found enemies, the military presented three unimaginative and underdeveloped options. Gen. Hugh Shelton, the chairman of the Joint Chiefs of Staff, was scheduled to retire at the end of the month and be replaced by Vice Chairman Gen. Richard Myers. Since the president had not provided the military with specific objectives, Shelton and Myers only came prepared with three "broad choices." The first option, deemed "Clintonian" due to its risk-averse nature, focused on launching cruise missile strikes against static—and most likely empty—al Qaeda targets. The second option, only a minor improvement from the first, combined cruise missile strikes with manned aircraft to increase the destructive capacity. The third option integrated the air campaign of the second option with the insertion of special operations units, followed closely by conventional ground troops. This third option interested the president, probably because it was the only serious option for retaliation and possessed symmetry to the CIA's extensive proposal. As Gen. Shelton later recalled, "Nothing was decided, although it was obvious that nobody would be backing options one or two."[39] Rumsfeld, still fixated on military transformation, emphasized the importance of speed and technology, although Shelton and Myers noted that both the Taliban and al Qaeda maintained few targetable assets vulnerable to America's advanced technological stockpile. Nonetheless, the military plan necessitated a tremendous diplomatic push for basing, staging, and overflight rights from neighboring countries, as well as iterative military planning; the most optimistic timetable required ten to twelve days to get the first boots on the ground.[40]

After the presentations, those at the meeting expressed concerns about the upcoming conflict. Defense Secretary Rumsfeld posed the problem of matching the priority to destroy al Qaeda with the objective of killing bin Laden. Rumsfeld believed that expressing the desire and establishing the objective of killing bin Laden might elevate his stature in the Muslim world and create the perception that the outcome of the war depended on his death or capture. The Soviet experience in Afghanistan disturbed Condoleezza Rice, the president's national security advisor. Given Afghanistan's complexity, ethnic distribution, and terrain, Rice said, "We are going to wish this was the Balkans."[41] Powell expressed the need for an international coalition, but the president countered that the United States would act unilaterally if necessary. When the meeting reconvened later that day, Rumsfeld articulated the need for military transformation. Directed at the military leadership, Rumsfeld said, "The military options look like five or ten years ago" and the military must prepare for a long, global, sustained campaign.[42] Rumsfeld understood the amorphous nature of al Qaeda, the challenge of deterring it, the lack of good targets and intelligence, and the importance of its ideology.[43] But his focus on al Qaeda's global disposition, combined with his fixation with military transformation, seemed to distract him from the war at hand. To him, Afghanistan was only one front in the overall campaign, and bin Laden was only one man.

Two days after hearing the options from his most senior advisors, the president outlined the shape of the upcoming war in Afghanistan. To Rumsfeld's dismay, the CIA received every authority that Tenet requested. The presidential order authorized the Agency to use all resources—including drones, lethal force, covert action, financial disruption, and intelligence collection—to defeat al Qaeda in Afghanistan. Bush wanted bin Laden "dead or alive," and that message trickled down the chain of command. Powell would issue an ultimatum to the Taliban to apprehend and extradite bin Laden through Pakistan. The president ordered the military to initiate and develop the third option that combined airpower with special operations forces, followed by conventional troops.

But even as the president issued commands, he still had not clarified the policy objectives for the campaign. According to President Bush, "Our goal is not to destroy the Taliban, but that may be the effect."[44] Two days before, Bush had said that "the ideal result from this campaign would be to kick terrorists out . . . [of] Afghanistan and through that action persuade other countries . . . to change their behavior."[45] At Camp David, Tenet and Powell met little resistance when they advocated directing American power to destroy the Taliban's military structure, not their leadership. The president's principal advisors agreed that killing or capturing bin Laden inflated his importance and therefore constituted an objective mismatch.[46] Rumsfeld later recalled, "Though I was eager to see them [Osama bin Laden and Mullah Omar] in American custody or dead, I knew the war would not end with their capture or deaths."[47] For all the parties involved, but particularly the military, the ambiguity of the objectives inhibited the formation of a clear, unified, and coherent strategy for the war in Afghanistan.

On September 18, just one week after the terrorist attacks, President Bush officially authorized the general war strategy for Afghanistan assembled over the past seven days. Responsibility for developing and executing it fell to Gen. Tommy Franks, the leader of Central Command (CENTCOM), the geographically-organized military command that oversees operations in the Middle East, North Africa, and Central Asia.[48] At the same time, the president asked Armitage to assemble a team to travel to Moscow to secure Russian support for the impending conflict. Afghanistan lay in Russia's sphere of influence, bordered on the north by the former Soviet republics of Turkmenistan, Uzbekistan, and Tajikistan. CTC chief Cofer Black traveled with Armitage to meet with Russian intelligence officials. The Russians possessed substantial intelligence and expertise as a result of their prolonged occupation of Afghanistan. The Russian leaders hesitated to provide full cooperation and support to Armitage's team, but Putin overruled them, marking the beginning of a long and fruitful counterterrorism relationship.[49]

In the first week after the September 11 terrorist attacks, the president and his national security team developed a multiagency strategy that combined advanced and unconventional methods of national power to defeat al Qaeda. But the intermediate objectives—the path to this vague end—remained nebulous. According to General Myers, "the definition of winning eluded us in the early parts of our campaign against the terrorists."[50] The CIA dominated American expertise on Afghanistan, but the military remained responsible for the overall strategy. Rumsfeld's fixation on quick and decisive projections of power further constrained the military, which already faced enormous pressure to respond quickly. Although the strategy was developed in a rushed and disorganized manner without clear intermediate objectives, the fundamental operational concept of generating a rapid response by joint interagency teams directing close air support, followed closely by conventional forces, appealed to the senior leadership in Washington.

3

PREPARING FOR WAR

September 19 to October 6, 2001

We would be the insurgents.

— GARY BERNTSEN[1]

Inside the counterterrorism chief's office at the CIA on September 19, 2001, Cofer Black put on another memorable performance. Just five days earlier, he had requested senior CIA operations officer Gary Schroen to lead the first team into Afghanistan. A career operative with multiple tours in Afghanistan and Pakistan, Schroen had entered a ninety-day transition to retirement just days before the 9/11 attacks. Now Schroen and his team of seven, code-named "Jawbreaker," prepared to spearhead the war effort. Schroen and his deputy, "Rick" (an alias), entered Black's office at 1 p.m., their last scheduled meeting before departing for Afghanistan. In his dramatic manner, Black issued orders on behalf of the president: ally with the Northern Alliance, establish a safe location for the insertion of SOF, and kill—not capture—bin Laden and his leadership. "They must be killed. I want to see photos of their heads on pikes. I want bin Laden's head shipped back in a box filled with dry ice. . . . Have I made myself clear?"[2]

CENTCOM commander Tommy Franks briefed Rumsfeld, Shelton, and Myers about the military's war concept on September 20. The blueprint contained four phases. Phase I aimed to "Set Conditions and Build Forces to Provide the National Command Authority Credible Military Options." As the DOD deployed troops to the theater of conflict, the CIA's paramilitary teams would establish relationships with anti-Taliban resistance while the State

Department pursued aggressive diplomacy. Franks labeled Phase II "Conduct Initial Operations and Continue to Set Conditions for Follow-on Operations." During this phase, SOF would enter Afghanistan and liaise with Afghan opposition forces to direct aerial attacks with precision ordnance. Phase III, titled "Conduct Decisive Combat Operations in Afghanistan, Continue to Build the Coalition, and Conduct Operations AOR [Area of Responsibility] Wide," embodied Rumsfeld's influence.[3] The concept seemed to indicate a desire to conduct decisive operations in Afghanistan and then move on to other areas, destroying al Qaeda country by country in a show of global power and reach. Phase IV, however, required the military to "Establish Capability of Coalition Partners to Prevent the Re-Emergence of Terrorism and Provide Support for Humanitarian Assistance Efforts." Both Rumsfeld and Bush resisted what they called nation-building but Myers "wasn't at all sure that we could topple the Taliban and eradicate al-Qaida and then simply leave."[4] Therefore, they relegated the responsibility for postwar Afghanistan to coalition partners.

The world watched as the president addressed a joint session of Congress on the night of September 20. Bush demanded that the Taliban immediately extradite the leaders of al Qaeda in Afghanistan and permanently close all terrorist training camps. In a famous declaration later termed "The Bush Doctrine," the president articulated the broad scope of America's efforts: "Our war on terror begins with al Qaeda, but it does not end there. It will not end until every terrorist group of global reach has been found, stopped, and defeated."[5] Bush tried to prepare the public that the impending conflict would not mirror the decisive nature of the Gulf War but rather unfold as a lengthy campaign using every aspect of national power to defeat terrorism and protect the United States. Despite Bush's unilateral inclination, he invited all nations to join America in a coalition for the global war on terror. The speech concluded the internal White House debate over the scope of the war. The United States was not waging a war against al Qaeda nor the Taliban; it was a "war on terror."

The next day, the Taliban formally rejected the president's demands, and all indications pointed to war. Just hours before, General Franks reluctantly met with the service chiefs—the top uniformed leaders of the Army, Navy, Air Force, and Marine Corps—to brief them on the war concept. With Rumsfeld's support already secured, Franks perceived this meeting as a formality ripe with the potential for leaks. But the service chiefs considered this their opportunity to provide advice for the war that they would soon resource and support. Suggestions and criticism came from all directions. Franks deemed the comments "parochial bullshit" to promote each service's advantage at the expense of the other.[6] Yet most of the arguments did not necessarily reflect inter-service rivalries but rather substantive debates: the Army demanded more troops, the Air Force desired primacy in bombing support, and the Navy wanted to position more carriers in the Persian Gulf. General Shelton viewed the feedback as "no big deal. . . . [B]y the time you walked out of there—if you had listened to what the service chiefs—each one an expert in the capabilities of his services—were suggesting, ultimately you would end up with a far superior plan."[7] But in the middle of the discussion, when one of the service chiefs expressed concern that the proposal would fail, Franks responded, "Bullshit. It's my plan. And I'm responsible for its execution," abruptly leaving the room and ending the meeting.[8] Later that day, Franks demanded that the service chiefs provide all "service expertise" through the three-star generals commanding a service component at CENTCOM.[9] By walking out of the briefing, the four-star general responsible for planning and executing America's war isolated himself from the service chiefs, some of the most experienced leaders in the military who prepared America's air, land, and sea power for every conflict.

After the unpleasant experience with the service chiefs, Franks met with Bush, Vice President Richard Cheney, Rumsfeld, Shelton, Myers, and Maj. Gen. Dell Dailey, the commander of Task Force Sword, to discuss CENTCOM's war concept. Franks briefed the room on the operational concept and Dailey outlined how the use of special operations forces—such as Navy SEALs, Army special operations forces, Green Berets, and Rangers—corresponded with Franks's proposal. The president asked about securing overflight, basing, and staging rights in neighboring countries. The military needed access to large bases in order to mass its troops before entering Afghanistan, maintain headquarters for command and control, and establish combat search-and-rescue (CSAR) capability for downed aircrews and embroiled soldiers. Pakistan acceded to American demands two days after 9/11, but Musharraf nonetheless hesitated to sanction an overt and massive buildup of American troops on his soil due to the prevalence of Islamic fundamentalism and anti-Americanism in Pakistan. Uzbekistan seemed likely to offer the best alternative, but the diplomatic process was moving slowly. In a statement conveying the overall war objective toward the end of the meeting, the president equated the Taliban with al Qaeda and called for the destruction of both. Franks considered this "one of the most direct and decisive statements of policy I had ever heard."[10] But by not differentiating between the two organizations, the president may have given Franks the impression that defeating the Taliban was as important as destroying al Qaeda.

Indeed, that distinction was the subject of some debate. Later that day, the president met with "the principals"—his core group of cabinet-level advisors—to discuss the future of the Taliban. Powell supported a targeted campaign that focused on al Qaeda and bypassed the Taliban, while Rice indicated that removing the Taliban from power protected American and Afghan interests. Backed by a recent field assessment from the CIA's chief of station in Pakistan, Tenet argued that concentrating on al Qaeda might encourage the Taliban leadership to separate from the terrorist organization to protect its own interests. To avoid widespread indigenous resistance to the American presence, the CIA and DOD wanted to spin the war as Afghans against foreign Arab demagogues. To pursue this strategy, however, meant bolstering anti-Taliban Afghan forces with as few American troops as possible. This economical method aligned with the CIA's historical experience with covert operations as well as the Agency's specific capabilities in Afghanistan. It also conformed to Rumsfeld's transformation concept of quick, decisive action with few post-conflict responsibilities. The military, conscious of the degree of risk, appreciated the minimization of danger for American troops. In short, this concept mitigated most of the principals' concerns about the war. The Soviets had sent hundreds of thousands of troops to Afghanistan only to withdraw from the bloody conflict after ten years. A light American footprint to strengthen an organic Afghan resistance movement seemed like the appropriate strategy for the circumstances. Bush concluded, "This should be the template for our strategy. We should use the Afghans in the struggle."[11]

The conversation then turned to the challenge of establishing basing rights and CSAR capability in Uzbekistan. The eighty-five-mile border between Uzbekistan and Afghanistan provided the best opportunity to establish a supply route into the Northern Alliance strongholds, particularly Mazar-i-Sharif. But negotiations stalled over using Karshi Khanabad (K2), a former Soviet base in southeastern Uzbekistan. Uzbekistan wanted to establish clear expectations for basing and staging rights, even though DOD itself lacked a well-defined plan that identified the specific equipment, resources, and number of personnel for mobilization. But the principals considered Uzbekistan bases a crucial factor for waging the war, and negotiations continued.[12]

The CSAR requirement epitomized the military's aversion to risk. Any military decision to execute an operation balances the inherent risk of that operation with its contingency plans. The Taliban possessed only a few aircraft and a primitive air defense and radar system. With a few dozen cruise-missile strikes, the United States could control the skies above Afghanistan. But despite air supremacy, somewhere along the military planning process the decision was made that establishing CSAR would be a prerequisite for military action.[13] CSAR provided the military with the means of mitigating risk during operations. According to Gen. James Mattis, who as a brigadier general commanded the first Marines to enter Afghanistan, "You have to have a way of getting your people out. You generally don't put people in where we can't get them out."[14]

Over the next week, the CSAR issue paralyzed American war efforts. President Bush wanted to start the campaign on October 2, but that date appeared increasingly unrealistic as it approached. Oman would provide CSAR bases for southern Afghanistan, and the aircraft carrier USS *Kitty Hawk* would operate as a staging base in the Persian Gulf. But by September 28, the entire strategy for the war in Afghanistan seemed to depend on establishing a CSAR capability in Uzbekistan. The president wanted to know the contingency plan if Uzbekistan denied access to K2. Rumsfeld replied, "If we have no CSAR in the north you can't have air operations in the north. Just in the south."[15] But the crux of the joint interagency plan focused on bolstering the Northern Alliance with close air support. There was no plan for southern Afghanistan because no substantial anti-Taliban force existed there.

The military's insistence on CSAR had acquired profound policy implications and reflected its institutional aversion to risk. The uniformed military leadership seemed unequivocal in its reluctance to undertake air operations without the capacity to rescue its people promptly. Contrary to military doctrine, this risk aversion sacrificed operational success for force protection. Furthermore, Secretary of Defense Rumsfeld allowed the military's resistance to risk to affect the policy-planning process and potentially cripple the current war plans. America's military leaders now held Operation Enduring Freedom hostage until CSAR capabilities were established. And despite Rumsfeld's authoritarian style and President Bush's exasperation with the delays, no civilian leader asserted control and overruled the military's hesitation.

At the same time as the CSAR dilemma, the military faced setbacks in targeting due to the lack of intelligence and in-country personnel. The Taliban maintained little infrastructure, and al Qaeda essentially possessed none. With neither enemy susceptible to bombing, the war almost necessitated troops on the ground in Afghanistan to identify more tactical targets. On September 26, the president wanted to give the military the go-ahead to start air operations in Afghanistan, but the military responded that not enough targets existed for an effective campaign. Bush found the response unacceptable but could do little to change it. By September 28, the targeting list approached seven hundred, mostly static Taliban targets and a few empty al Qaeda training camps. The next day Rumsfeld somberly reported to the group, "The target list cannot impose much damage on the people we want to impose it on." Myers agreed: "You're not going to topple a regime with this target list."[16] Indeed, the assumption that airpower could act as the decisive element to overthrow the Taliban reflected not only a misunderstanding of the nature of the enemy but a fundamental misreading of the historical role of airpower in war. Between the lack of targets and the inability to establish CSAR and insert SOF, the weaknesses of the war concept began to show.

Meanwhile, Gary Schroen and his Jawbreaker team arrived in the Panjshir Valley of northern Afghanistan on September 26. The CIA detachment collaborated closely with Gen. Mohammed Fahim, who led the Northern Alliance after Massoud's death on September 9. The insertion of SOF to laser-designate targets for bombing was intended to follow closely, but these follow-on operations would be delayed for three weeks due to the CSAR conundrum and poor weather. The CIA operatives worked quickly and effectively to build relationships with key leaders of the anti-Taliban resistance, distribute large sums of cash, acquire and disseminate intelligence, and identify targets. Over the next thirty days, Schroen and his team produced over four hundred intelligence reports.[17] As the first Americans into Afghanistan after September 11, the Jawbreaker team was operating in hostile territory without CSAR, contingency plans, or air support.

The stalemate in initiating military action broke on October 3 when Uzbekistan finally agreed to CSAR, staging, and basing rights at K2. Schroen issued his first field appraisal from Afghanistan, highlighting the importance of aerial attacks on the Taliban front lines with the Northern Alliance to enable the anti-Taliban factions to break out from the stalemate. Most importantly, the principals in the White House finally reached a consensus and agreed on overthrowing the Taliban as the proper objective for Afghanistan. The air campaign would begin on the night of October 7, and SOF would deploy into Afghanistan soon after. Although the war effort had progressed rapidly from its conceptualization during the days after 9/11, much remained unresolved.[18]

The decision to overthrow the Taliban regime followed three weeks of limited and ultimately unsuccessful attempts to break the Taliban from al Qaeda. Just after 9/11, top-level U.S. officials met with director general of the ISI Mahmud Ahmed in order to ask him to persuade Mullah Omar to sever its relationship with al Qaeda and turn bin Laden over to the United States.[19] Mahmud, who only days earlier had provided CIA Deputy Director John McLaughlin with a "very positive portrayal" of Mullah Omar, reluctantly traveled to Kandahar and met privately with the Taliban leader.[20] According to former White House advisor Bruce Riedel:

> What they said remains unknown. Mahmud later told Shuja Nawaz that he felt he could not press Omar to hand over a fellow Muslim. Even if Mahmud did try to convince Omar to do so, perhaps he failed because his heart was not in the mission. He may have actually told him to hang tough and fight. Mahmud told the CIA station chief [in Pakistan], Bob Grenier, that he found it distasteful to betray the Taliban to America when Washington had betrayed Pakistan and adhered to the Pressler Amendment [that imposed harsh sanctions on Pakistan due to its nuclear weapons program]. Mahmud may well have proposed that the Taliban make a half-hearted show of appeasing America's anger because he did not want to abandon the course the army and ISI had been following in Afghanistan for more than a decade.[21]

Amb. Zalmay Khalilzad, who at the time was the director for Southwest Asia on the National Security Council, also indicated that Mahmud unenthusiastically encouraged Mullah Omar to cooperate with U.S. demands:

It's clear that with regard to the overthrow of the Taliban, Pakistan did not resist. I think it's likely to have encouraged the Taliban leadership to cooperate with the U.S. before the attack. But in fact . . . one of the ISI leaders [Mahmud Ahmed] was sent by President Musharraf to talk to Mullah Omar and to say that the U.S. is serious and that he ought to cooperate by distancing the Taliban from [al Qaeda] or perhaps turning over al Qaeda figures. But while he passed that message on, there were reports that he said that his personal view was that they should not take that action. Perhaps, that's why this ISI leader was replaced.[22]

Omar convened a two-day meeting with his leadership to determine the Taliban's response. Ultimately, the Taliban leader stayed true to his words from March 2001: "Half of my country has been destroyed by two decades of war. If the remaining half is also destroyed in trying to protect Mr. bin Laden, I am willing for this sacrifice."[23]

Around the same time that ISI Director Mahmud met with Mullah Omar, CIA station chief Bob Grenier traveled to the Balochistan region of Pakistan to meet with Mullah Akhtar Mohammad Osmani, arguably the second most powerful leader of the Taliban. Grenier proposed a variety of options surrounding the concept that the Taliban would split from al Qaeda and turn bin Laden over to the United States for prosecution. Osmani returned to Kandahar and passed the message along to Mullah Omar, who rejected the American proposals. On October 2, Grenier met again with Osmani in Baluchistan and suggested that Osmani overthrow Omar, betray al Qaeda, and thus protect the Taliban from America's wrath. This attempt also proved unsuccessful.[24]

All American efforts to split the Taliban from al Qaeda failed. After the start of military operations, the CIA recommended pursuing a limited air campaign in southern Afghanistan so as not to alienate Pashtuns and therefore create fissures within the Taliban. A CIA team also met with Abdul Haq Wasiq, the deputy director of intelligence for the Taliban, in enemy territory outside of Kabul to try to get the Taliban to turn over bin Laden. When the official indicated that he would do no such thing, the CIA team rolled him up in a carpet and drove him in the back of a truck to a secure area for questioning. Wasiq would stay in American custody for the duration of the campaign and was in the first batch of prisoners transferred to the Guantanamo Bay detention facilities in early 2002, where he remains as of 2013. In the end, both operations failed to drive a wedge between the Taliban and al Qaeda.[25] Nonetheless, the decision to pursue regime change in Afghanistan implied that the United States would be responsible for replacing the Taliban with another government. At the NSC meeting on October 4, Bush queried the principals on the plan for a post-Taliban Afghanistan. Nobody provided an adequate answer.[26]

At the operational level, the military's war concept was designed to create a "kill box" between the four cities of Mazar-i-Sharif, Taloqan, Kabul, and Bamiyan. Strategically located near K2 in Uzbekistan, Mazar-i-Sharif was pivotal to establishing a land bridge and supply route for U.S. forces. Therefore, Northern Alliance forces in Mazar-i-Sharif would capture the city and then proceed eastward toward Taloqan to unite with Northern Alliance forces on the Shomali Plains. After capturing Taloqan, the Northern Alliance would move south to Kabul and then west to Bamiyan, trapping the Taliban and al Qaeda in a lopsided square in northeastern Afghanistan. AC-130 gunships would patrol the major passes within the kill box to eliminate the enemy and prevent retreating forces from reinforcing the Taliban front lines in the south.[27]

However, it would be the CIA that would initially spearhead such operations. In contrast to the military's war concepts, CTC director Cofer Black and his deputy Hank Crumpton had devised a forceful plan to topple the Taliban and attack al Qaeda in Afghanistan. Gary Berntsen, who would take over for Gary Schroen as the top CIA field officer in Afghanistan at the end of October, argued that the CIA masterminded the war effort. At that time, he was in a unique position to observe the differences between the plans of attack formulated by the CIA and those of the military, as well as the implementation of those strategies. Bertnsen later recalled,

> Cofer Black and Hank Crumpton were the architects of the campaign. . . . These guys had the plan, they had laid this thing out, they knew exactly what they were going to do, brought me back, sat me down, and laid out the plan. . . .
>
> They were going to create approximately four to six teams. They were going to be led each of them by a case officer. The deputy chief of each of those teams would be a paramilitary officer. They'd have a mix of linguists, a mix of case officers, and that we would be the insurgents. And

we would not have a large target for them to attack on the ground. We would leverage existing relationships with warlords, and we would conduct a guerrilla campaign against them [the Taliban] in the beginning and bring firepower to bear with them.

This was all done on day one when I walked through the door. . . . And this was very, very early. I met with Cofer and he also had the same vision of this. . . . Cofer was dealing with the politics of Washington, D.C., dealing with the White House and with the National Security Council. So, the first thing to understand is those are the two architects of the campaign.[28]

But as the United States prepared to go to war, the extent to which the phases and concepts developed by the military were part of a broader war plan remains unclear. The four phases that General Franks presented to the war cabinet on September 20 were merely a standard template for the conduct of any war and had little substantive value. There is no available evidence to suggest that the initial preparations for war went much beyond these phases and basic operational concepts, although most official documentation remains classified. On the contrary, CIA officer Gary Berntsen maintains that while General Franks had some documents and a conceptual understanding for a plan of attack, no real war plan existed.[29] Deputy CIA Director John McLaughlin also concluded that the war plan was both unconventional and somewhat improvisational.[30] And since the president had not yet decided upon clear objectives achievable through military force, it was inconceivable that the military could develop an adequate war plan before receiving its instructions. When Franks stated that he needed two months to devise a war plan for Afghanistan, Rumsfeld responded, "General, I'm afraid we don't have that much time" and instructed Franks to develop the "first cut of a plan" in a few days.[31] Nonetheless, Rumsfeld expressed his frustration with the result and intended to tell the president, "Even before you hear the plan, I want to state: You will find it disappointing. I did."[32]

Seven days after General Franks briefed the war cabinet on the four phases, President Bush's patience with the lack of a war plan expired. According to Condoleezza Rice,

The military planning was proceeding smoothly but slowly, and the President was getting frustrated. It seemed that every NSC meeting ended inconclusively, with the military not quite ready to present a plan to the President. . . .

Finally the President's patience ran out. I'd gone to the CIA for a briefing on the afternoon of September 27. I was called out of the meeting to take a call from the President. He was clearly agitated. "I want a plan tomorrow," he said. "Call Don, and make sure I have one." . . .

I called Don immediately and told him about my discussions with the President. "Don, he's had it." I said. "There really needs to be a final plan tomorrow." "Got it," Don answered. . . .

Don delivered the next morning with a very good presentation of a final plan for the President's approval. I was relieved, though already the tendency of the Pentagon to give military briefings that were lacking in detail was evident. . . .

Don was resistant to a review of the actual battle plan with the NSC Principals, relying instead on briefings with the President that were sometimes short on operational details.[33]

In the end, the U.S. military had eight days—from September 20 to 28—to turn four generic phases for war into a comprehensive and executable war plan. Most U.S. war plans, such as OPLAN 1003 for the invasion of Iraq, contain hundreds of pages detailing deployments, logistics, and complex operations. Furthermore, President Bush had not yet provided the U.S. military with specific objectives to accomplish during the campaign. General Franks had even communicated to Rumsfeld that developing an adequate war plan for Afghanistan would take two months. In this context, it seems nearly impossible that the documents presented to the president on September 28 constituted a genuine war plan.

Less than one month after being attacked, the United States of America began to respond militarily. Conventional wars—the type that bin Laden expected—typically require months to develop a war plan, build up an adequate number of troops in theater, engage in coercive diplomacy, and build a coalition. The innovative use of joint interagency teams to direct precision-guided munitions and support Afghan resistance forces enabled America to act in weeks, not months.

Still, the planning process had its flaws. The lack of intelligence on al Qaeda, the Taliban, and Afghanistan, as well as the nature of the enemy, resulted in a limited target list. The military's intrinsic risk aversion delayed the beginning of war and influenced the desire to minimize the use of American soldiers and maximize the use of indigenous Afghan forces. And America's military commander responsible for the war effort isolated himself from the very members of the military he depended on most. The absence of clear objectives permeated every level of the war effort. Ultimately, the decisions made during the war-planning process in late September and early October, along with the lack of an adequate war plan, shaped the future of the war effort in Afghanistan.

4

A SLOW START

October 7 to October 18, 2001

No one starts a war—or rather, no one in his senses ought to do so—
without first being clear in his mind what he intends to achieve by that
war and how he intends to conduct it. The former is its political
purpose; the latter is its operational objective. This is the governing
principle which will set its course, prescribe the scale of means and
effort which is required, and make its influence felt throughout down
to the smallest operational detail.

— CARL VON CLAUSEWITZ, ON WAR[1]

On October 7, 2001, President Bush announced the beginning of military operations in Afghanistan. But the objectives for Operation Enduring Freedom (OEF) were still nebulous. In his public address, the president stated that OEF sought to "disrupt the use of Afghanistan as a terrorist base of operations, and to attack the military capability of the Taliban regime."[2] President Bush later said, "Removing al Qaeda's safe haven in Afghanistan was essential to protecting the American people."[3]

Soon after the president's speech, Rumsfeld and Myers gave their first wartime press briefing in the Pentagon. Both Bush and Rumsfeld indicated that the military would focus on limiting Afghanistan's viability as a free base of operations for terrorists. Rumsfeld described the six primary objectives of the military operation:

♦ To make clear to the Taliban leaders and their supporters that harboring terrorists is unacceptable and carries a price.

43

- To acquire intelligence to facilitate future operations against al Qaeda and the Taliban regime that harbors the terrorists.
- To develop relationships with groups in Afghanistan that oppose the Taliban regime and the foreign terrorists that they support.
- To make it increasingly difficult for the terrorists to use Afghanistan freely as a base of operation.
- To alter the military balance over time by denying to the Taliban the offensive systems that hamper the progress of the various opposition forces.
- And to provide humanitarian relief to Afghans suffering truly oppressive living conditions under the Taliban regime.[4]

National Security Advisor Condoleezza Rice echoed the goals that the president and defense secretary declared at the press briefings. According to Rice, "this meant destroying camps, disrupting communications, and driving targets out of their safe havens to bring them to justice."[5] Deputy National Security Advisor Stephen Hadley stated, "The purpose of the operation [Enduring Freedom] was to eliminate Afghanistan as a safe haven for al Qaeda, and dismantle al Qaeda's operations there."[6] Yet neither the president nor his cabinet indicated that defeating al Qaeda was the primary objective.

The top three officials at the Department of Defense had much broader and more ambitious objectives in mind. To these individuals, the strategic goal was to "prevent further terrorist attacks against the US or US interests."[7] According to Secretary Rumsfeld, "We wanted to not only destroy al-Qaida in Afghanistan, but to cause al-Qaida and its affiliates everywhere to scramble for cover, to coerce their sponsors to sever their ties with them, and to persuade our allies and friends to join us in our efforts."[8] Deputy Secretary of Defense Paul Wolfowitz and Under Secretary of Defense Douglas Feith concurred. Feith later stated,

Our primary goal was not retaliation but preventing the next attack. It is hard to overstate how significant, radical, and ambitious that was. . . . We concluded that these groups benefited greatly from some sort of base of operations to conduct large operations. And because key parts of the networks were invisible to us, we intended to hit the visible parts in the hopes of causing disruption to the entire network. . . . We [therefore] focused on state supporters of terrorism. If you think that 9/11 led inevitably to our military action in Afghanistan, then you aren't doing justice to the administration's strategic deliberations.[9]

In their eyes, the fundamental enabling factor for international terrorism was state sponsorship. Operation Enduring Freedom therefore sought to remove Afghanistan as a haven for terrorist organizations and send a signal to state sponsors of terrorism that sponsorship would not be tolerated. Al Qaeda and Afghanistan were simply manifestations of a larger, global phenomenon. Indeed, Afghanistan was, in Rumsfeld's words, the "opening salvo" of a wider campaign against terrorism.[10]

Within the U.S. military, the absence of clear objectives resulted in competing and varying visions for the execution of Operation Enduring Freedom. According to Chairman of the Joint Chiefs of Staff Richard Myers, the primary objective was to "capture or kill as many al Qaeda as we could."[11] General Myers viewed the Taliban as a subordinate obstacle to this goal. Lt. Gen. Michael DeLong, the deputy commander of CENTCOM, saw three basic objectives for Operation Enduring Freedom: "wipe out al-Qaeda in Afghanistan, rid the country of Taliban leadership, and help the Afghan populace by setting up infrastructure, hospitals, and providing humanitarian aid."[12] Col. John Mulholland, the commander of the Fifth Special Forces Group in Afghanistan, considered the larger goal to be to "overthrow the Taliban regime and remove Afghanistan as a sanctuary for al Qaeda."[13] Brig. Gen. James Mattis, the commander of the first Marine contingent in Afghanistan, viewed the primary objective to be to "make sure that the enemy didn't feel like they had any safe haven, to destroy their sense of security in southern Afghanistan, to isolate Kandahar from its lines of communication, and to move against Kandahar."[14]

At the Central Intelligence Agency, Director George Tenet indicated that the CIA aimed to "strangle their [al Qaeda's] safe haven in Afghanistan, seal the borders, go after the leadership, shut off their money, and pursue al-Qa'ida in ninety-two countries around the world."[15] Indeed, CIA officials generally had a more narrow view of the objectives for the U.S. war in Afghanistan than the broad, vague, and expansive goals set forth by their counterparts in the Department of Defense. According to Tenet's deputy John McLaughlin,

> The objective was pretty simple for [Operation] Enduring Freedom. It was to defeat the Taliban, to capture and kill or drive out as many al Qaeda as we could, and to destroy Afghanistan's value as a safe haven for al Qaeda—basically, to change the geopolitical circumstances that had made 9/11 possible.[16]

Gary Berntsen, who would succeed Gary Schroen as the top CIA field officer in Afghanistan, explained the objectives of the campaign in the following way:

> The Taliban have not agreed [to turn over bin Laden]. They will be in the way. Eliminate as many of them as you can. Kill them all. They are in front of you. Eliminate them. If they will negotiate with you, negotiate with them. If you can turn them, turn them. If not, kill them all. When it comes to al Qaeda, identify them and eliminate them as quickly as you can. Your orders are to kill bin Laden and eliminate every one of them.[17]

Deputy CTC Director Hank Crumpton described three similar strategic objectives: "First, we must destroy AQ leadership. Second, we must deny them safe haven. Third, we must attack the political-social-economic conditions the enemy exploits."[18]

At the State Department, Deputy Secretary Richard Armitage viewed the objectives as eliminating al Qaeda and removing the Taliban as a governing force.[19] Amb. James Dobbins, who would become the special envoy to the Afghan Resistance and broker the post-Taliban political agreement in Germany in late 2001, concurred with Armitage. According to Ambassador Dobbins, the primary objectives were to "displace the Taliban government, replace it with a more acceptable, more cooperative, more moderate, more internationally minded successor, and hunt down, capture, or kill remaining al Qaeda targets within the country."[20]

The absence of unanimity over the objectives for Operation Enduring Freedom reflected a lack of unified strategic vision that would ultimately enable al Qaeda to continue its existence in the region. While most of the civilian and military leaders recognized that al Qaeda and the Taliban were the enemies, a clear and unified understanding of how to defeat these adversaries never emerged. The president and his immediate subordinates considered the primary objective to be to remove Afghanistan as a haven for terrorism. Despite the eagerness to kill as many terrorists as possible, operations were structured around regime change first and consequentially expelling al Qaeda from Afghanistan. But displacing al Qaeda was not synonymous with victory. The presence of vast, ungoverned spaces in neighboring Pakistan offered the terrorists a newfound sanctuary beyond the reach of American forces. So as the United States began its war in Afghanistan, it fought not to destroy al Qaeda decisively, but rather to disperse an already decentralized enemy. And this critical, seemingly simple distinction greatly affected military operational choices.

American bombs and cruise missiles began to descend on Afghanistan on the night of October 7. But instead of a resolute show of American air supremacy, the first strikes in Afghanistan seemed lackluster and anticlimactic. Despite forty thousand military personnel and 393 aircraft dedicated to the operation, the military struck only thirty-one targets with fifty cruise missiles, fifteen bombers, and twenty-five other aircraft. The targets consisted mostly of low-value, static but strategic locations, such as the primitive Taliban air defense systems and empty al Qaeda camps. No ordnance hit the Taliban front lines with the Northern Alliance. Nor was bin Laden targeted. Worse, initial reports showed that the attack had missed three leadership targets. The next day's bomb damage assessment revealed that many targets remained unscathed. During the preceding week, Schroen had prepared General Fahim and the Northern Alliance for a sustained and dedicated bombing campaign, but the meager effort of the first day dampened expectations.[21]

The bombing on the next day confirmed the lack of targets and actionable intelligence. Using seventy aircraft for 166 sorties, the aerial assault destroyed eleven radars, seven airfields, half of a long-range radar system, and some targets in Tora Bora. But Myers reported to the NSC, "Our TAC air [tactical aircraft] are loitering, waiting for emerging targets identified by the Predator."[22] In two days the military had exhausted much of its target list. The focus briefly turned to the mountainous region of Tora Bora, a well-known haven for bin Laden and his leadership. Myers stated that thirty-two two-thousand-pound bombs would descend on Tora Bora the next day. The diplomatic efforts, however, seemed to demonstrate positive results. In a show of commitment, President Musharraf dismissed Mahmud Ahmed, his intelligence chief, along with several other pro-Taliban leaders. Hamid Karzai also returned from Pakistan to his home in southern Afghanistan.[23]

Hamid Karzai would prove to be a significant figure in the future of Afghanistan. Karzai was born in 1957 in Kandahar to a prominent and respected Pashtun family. His father, Abdul Ahad Karzai, was chief of the Popalzai tribe and a former deputy speaker of parliament. After attending high school in Kabul and studying political science in northern India, Hamid Karzai worked as a spokesman and foreign policy advisor for a moderate anticommunist Afghan leader during the Soviet invasion. Karzai was an impassioned critic of the extremist factions of the mujahideen and the support that the ISI gave to such organizations. After the Soviets withdrew from Afghanistan, Karzai was arrested by Ahmad Shah Massoud's government and interrogated on the orders of then interior minister Mohammed Fahim. The National Directorate for Security building was shelled during Karzai's interrogation, and he managed to escape and flee to Peshawar. Karzai originally supported the Taliban as they rose to power but quickly reversed his stance: "They [the Taliban] were good people initially, but the tragedy was that very soon after they were taken over by the ISI and became a proxy."[24] To the displeasure of Mullah Omar and the ISI, the Karzai family began organizing against the Taliban from Quetta. In August 1999 the Taliban (with ISI assistance) assassinated Abdul Ahad Karzai as he exited a mosque, further invigorating his son's opposition to what the Taliban had become. Karzai continued to meet with leaders of the anti-Taliban opposition throughout 2001 in order to unite the disparate factions into a solitary movement. In the months preceding 9/11, the ISI informed Karzai that he was no longer welcome in Pakistan, presumably at the request of Mullah Omar.[25]

From the outside, Hamid Karzai was a charismatic and well-educated leader who was fluent in Pashto, Dari, Urdu, English, French, and Hindi, friendly with most Western governments, and most importantly an ethnic Pashtun. He also represented one of the few Pashtuns who had established positive relationships with the Northern Alliance and the rest of the anti-Taliban movement. These qualities made him a particularly appealing ally in America's war on terrorism because of his potential to rally resistance in the Taliban stronghold of southern Afghanistan. Indeed, Karzai would become the most important leader in the post-Taliban Afghanistan.

The days between the start of air operations and the insertion of special operations units became known to the staff at CENTCOM as the "ten days of hell." The lack of quality targets and intelligence did not improve, and pressure concentrated sharply on the military leadership to produce results and put boots on the ground. On October 9, bombers struck only thirteen targets. On October 10, Gary Schroen issued his second field appraisal, promoting the Northern Alliance as "the best fighting force in the country" and encouraging the American leadership to begin directing ordnance to the Taliban front lines.[26] By 2001, the Northern Alliance only controlled the northeastern corner of Afghanistan along with small pockets of territory dispersed across the north. The Northern Alliance occupied the strategic high ground, but neither it nor the Taliban had the military strength to break the stalemate at these front lines. With CSAR established at K2 in Uzbekistan, special operations units could finally deploy into Afghanistan and shift the military advantage in favor of the Northern Alliance. But the unforgiving weather in the mountains separating Uzbekistan from Afghanistan thwarted numerous insertion attempts.[27]

Rumsfeld interrogated Franks incessantly about the delays in inserting troops into Afghanistan. While weather was a limiting factor, Franks was also waiting for intelligence teams to deploy before infiltrating SOF to certain locations in Afghanistan. Rumsfeld was frustrated that Franks had not considered inserting SOF teams without intelligence liaisons, especially in the south where intelligence lacked significant relationships with anti-Taliban forces. Franks grew exasperated with what he perceived as Rumsfeld's harassment and micromanaging. During a conference call with the secretary of defense and Gen. Richard Myers, who had taken Hugh Shelton's place as chairman of the Joint Chiefs of Staff on October 1, Franks threatened to resign. A functional civil-military relationship depended on confidence and trust, and Franks felt that Rumsfeld no longer had confidence in him. But once Rumsfeld and Myers reaffirmed their support for Franks, operations resumed. Rumsfeld seemed to have learned his lesson and toned down his impatience and hostility to levels Franks found manageable.[28]

Under Secretary of Defense Douglas Feith later recounted the tensions during this period:

Rumsfeld had daily phone calls with General Franks. Franks at first would come on and start to talk to the secretary and give him a report. The secretary was very unhappy because he wasn't getting the information that he desired. Rumsfeld would ask quantitative questions, and Franks wouldn't have the answers. This would cause Rumsfeld to become annoyed, and in return Franks would become doubly annoyed. The mutual unhappiness in these early days was aggravated by the problems in sending in the [Special Forces] A-Teams. Day after day, Rumsfeld asked Franks when U.S. troops would be inserted into Afghanistan, and Franks would say, "I'm working on it." This bureaucratic answer infuriated Rumsfeld, while Franks was tearing his hair out from Rumsfeld's relentless pressure. As Franks related in his book, he told Rumsfeld that it appears that he would need to find a new commander. The problem was mitigated when Rumsfeld's staff came up with a form that Franks could use to give the quantitative elements of his report in writing to Rumsfeld before the daily phone calls. Rumsfeld would then get a piece of paper that anticipated a lot of his questions.[29]

Indeed, Secretary Rumsfeld was relentlessly engaged in the operational and tactical details during the ten days of hell. He exercised a high level of civilian control that bordered on micromanagement and expressed no reservations about doing so. Just as Rumsfeld had instructed in his collection of lessons for government leaders entitled "Rumsfeld's Rules," he reserved "the right to get into anything. . . . Although many responsibilities are delegated, no one should be surprised when the secretary engages an important issue."[30]

Rumsfeld's frustration with the military during these ten days was further captured in his October 10 memorandum to JCS chairman Myers and vice chairman Gen. Peter Pace titled "What Will Be the Military Role in the War on Terrorism?"

> For a month, DoD has produced next to no actionable suggestions as to how we can assist in applying the urgently needed pressure on terrorists other than cruise missiles and bombs.
>
> The American people are paying one-third of a trillion dollars per year for DoD. We have tens of thousands of dedicated, talented, creative people

who are anxious to be helpful in this international effort. But something is fundamentally wrong in the Department. Somewhere, between the President's repeated urgent requests and my strong and repeatedly expressed urgings, and the 1.5 million people in the Department, there is a complete disconnect. I am seeing next to nothing that is thoughtful, creative or actionable. How can that be? Is it because the Defense establishment has spent the last decade becoming increasingly risk adverse? . . .

All I can imagine is that down the line, in many locations in OSD [Office of the Secretary of Defense], the Joint Staff, and the CINCs [commanders in chiefs, also known as combatant commanders], there are middle-level people making terribly wrong judgments with respect to political risk and military risk, decisions they are not qualified to make and ought not to be making. They must be systematically dumbing down all proposals that anyone creative is coming up with to the point that they block every idea except cruise missiles and bombers. . . .

You must figure out a way for us to get this job done. You must find out what in the world the problem is and why DoD is such a persistent and unacceptably dry well.[31]

Secretary Rumsfeld struggled throughout the opening campaign of Operation Enduring Freedom to readjust the military's risk calculus. By the very nature of its responsibilities, the U.S. military faces the difficult task of determining what level of risk is acceptable for a given operation. Such calculations are based on numerous factors, including the importance of the operation, the potential benefits, and the contingency plans available if some aspect of the operation goes awry. The American military experiences in the Gulf War, Somalia, Haiti, Bosnia, and Kosovo had informed the way that the U.S. military thought about risk. During the 1990s the U.S. military focused heavily on protecting its soldiers and developing methods to prevent putting Americans in harm's way. U.S. military doctrine in these conflicts preached the use of overwhelming force and accepted relatively low levels of risk. As Rumsfeld's October 10 memo candidly reveals, this institutional pattern of risk aversion extended past the September 11 terrorist attacks. Of the three initial options that the military offered to the president at Camp David on September 15, only the third option put U.S. soldiers in direct danger. The other two focused on using cruise missiles and bombers to attack the Taliban and al Qaeda. And as the U.S. military worked to establish combat search and rescue for Afghanistan, the lack of CSAR initially threatened to preclude air operations in northern Afghanistan. Meanwhile, the Bush administration advocated a light-footprint strategy so as to avoid inciting violent Afghan resistance to the U.S. invasion. This military and civilian aversion to risk would have important consequences later in the campaign when U.S. government officials considered sending additional troops to Tora Bora.

On October 17 a special operations helicopter inserted an eight-person intelligence team near Mazar-i-Sharif to support Gen. Abdul Rashid Dostum, an ethnic Uzbek. But Uzbekistan and Tajikistan continued to refuse overflight clearance for special operations forces. This combined with poor weather conditions to prevent SOF units from slipping into Afghanistan.[32]

The lag between the beginning of the bombing campaign and the insertion of special operations forces weakened America's war effort in Afghanistan. The limited bombing campaign strained relations with anti-Taliban resistance factions, created uncertainty about U.S. resolve, and revitalized previously fearful enemies. The lack of actionable intelligence and salient targets resulted in a halfhearted air campaign that discouraged America's Afghan allies. Operations progressed slowly with only sixteen Americans in Afghanistan and no ability to immediately insert SOF. The discord between General Franks and Secretary Rumsfeld came close to shattering one of the most important relationships in the war. And the chaotic war-planning process failed to establish clear, adequate, and unified objectives, while the military failed to produce satisfactory war plan and continued to demonstrate its aversion to risk. It was far from an ideal start to the conflict.

5

THE STRATEGIC VOID

October 19 to November 2, 2001

Strategy is the key to warfare.

—ANTOINE-HENRI JOMINI[1]

The debate over Kabul highlighted the absence of any strategy for southern Afghanistan. The most consideration given to the Pashtun-dominated Taliban stronghold of southern Afghanistan came in the form of deciding whether or not the south would have any responsibilities in occupying Kabul. With little actionable intelligence, no organized resistance movement, incredibly unforgiving terrain, and substantial indigenous ideological support for the Taliban and al Qaeda, creating a strategy for southern Afghanistan represented a tremendous challenge. So the White House ignored it.[2]

During the ten days of hell at CENTCOM, the principals at the White House vigorously debated the future of Kabul and the best use for the Northern Alliance. Tenet and his field commander in Afghanistan, Gary Schroen, argued that American airpower should provide close air support for the Northern Alliance so that it could consolidate northern Afghanistan and take Kabul. Cheney agreed but reminded the advisors that the primary objective was al Qaeda. Yet the common aphorism "kill or capture bin Laden" had slowly degraded into "kill, capture, or put on the run." Powell expressed concern that supporting minority ethnic factions to take over the country's capital might alienate the majority Pashtuns, resulting in long-term political difficulties. He suggested that the UN could occupy Kabul until the political process offered an indigenous and democratic solution. Rumsfeld avoided the topic and focused on operations outside of Afghanistan.[3] As American warplanes flew over Afghanistan and special operations forces deployed into combat, the lack of a consensus at the White House left a void in the policy and strategy.

The operational impasse broke during the early hours of October 20. Poor weather gave way to clear skies, and the diplomatic effort succeeded in obtaining overflight permission from Uzbekistan and Tajikistan. Twelve-man teams of Green Berets, referred to as operational detachments alpha (ODAs), or A-teams, could finally enter Afghanistan. ODA 555, codenamed "Triple Nickel," deployed to the Panjshir Valley to join Schroen and his Jawbreaker team. ODA 595 arrived near Mazar-i-Sharif to attach to the other CIA team supporting General Dostum. At the same time, two hundred Army Rangers parachuted onto a landing strip sixty miles from Kandahar in southern Afghanistan. Codenamed Operation Rhino, the incursion claimed to show the American ability to strike anywhere in Afghanistan. But the operation secretly supported a much more important objective. U.S. special operations forces inserted into Afghanistan to raid Mullah Mohammed Omar's compound in Kandahar. Everyone expected the Taliban leader's home to be empty, but the mere ability to assault leadership targets with America's best soldiers represented a substantial improvement over previously established capabilities.[4]

Within the White House, the chaotic war-planning process increased strategic uncertainty. Despite the established chain of command that gave CENTCOM control over all CIA operations in Afghanistan, Rumsfeld felt that the CIA was running the show. At one NSC meeting, President Bush asked, "Who has the lead?"[5] Rumsfeld said, "This is the CIA's strategy. They developed the strategy. We're just executing the strategy."[6] John McLaughlin, the deputy director of the CIA, disagreed and stated that the in-country CIA units reported to Franks and simply prepared the way for the military. Armitage chimed in, calling the situation "FUBAR" (fucked up beyond all recognition).[7] According to Armitage,

> Mr. Rumsfeld asked Tommy Franks to do it [Operation Enduring Freedom] on the quick and . . . on the cheap. He didn't want to put a lot of forces on the ground. And it was rather uncoordinated . . . because we couldn't decide what Special Forces were going to do, what the CIA was going to do, who handed off to whom, who supported whom. So,

these things worked out on the ground. . . . We also unwittingly solved a lot of personal revenge scores for different Afghan factions. . . . After what I had heard between Tenet and Rumsfeld . . . I thought things were FUBAR . . . and that's, I think, indicative of the fact that we were a little messy.[8]

Deputy Director McLaughlin recalled the event in some detail:

The CIA was in the lead for a short while conceptually, but once you had American forces on the ground there, under the command of General Franks, the CENTCOM commander, at that point the military was in the lead. At the point when you blended CENTCOM and CIA, our view was that Tommy Franks was the commander and we were working for him. Now, it's always ambiguous and the CIA continues to work for the director of CIA, but the director of CIA was in close contact with the CENTCOM commander at this period in time. We would go down to Tampa, they would come up and see us. We would sit around a table and plan things together. But fundamentally, the CENTCOM commander owned this theater of war.

There's a famous scene in one of Woodward's books in which there is confusion about this in a Situation Room meeting where Secretary Rumsfeld points at me and says, "He's in charge," and I point back and say, "No, he's in charge," because it was our view that Tommy Franks was in command. And that scene is pretty accurately portrayed in that book. . . . Armitage says that this is all FUBAR, which I never liked because from our point of view it wasn't FUBAR—it was clear. It's just that it wasn't clearly understood in that room. But from our point of view, and at that point from Tommy Franks's point of view, it was quite clear.

This is one of the confusing things about this period in that Secretary Rumsfeld was a great war commander in Afghanistan, but at this moment in time I think the Pentagon leadership was still getting its arms around this problem. The CIA rushed right out to the CENTCOM commander, and I think that we had an understanding at the command level of how this was all working. And in the chaos of the times, I don't know that we had connected all the dots at the senior cabinet level in Washington. So it's not Rumsfeld's fault—it was just a chaotic period. He figured it out right away and said, "Okay, I'm in charge." He was not resisting being in charge, he was saying it's not clearly worked out bureaucratically here.[9]

At the highest levels of government, the Department of Defense was purportedly in the lead for Operation Enduring Freedom. However, the reality on the ground in Afghanistan did not necessarily reflect the established command structure in Washington. Rather, CIA teams often acted independently of the military and at many points performed political and military functions. According to CIA officer Gary Berntsen,

> We [the CIA teams in Afghanistan] dealt directly with the warlords, completely. We would keep the military advised of what we were doing, but I wasn't getting instructions [from the military]. I mean, I met with Franks. I was told that if Tommy Franks wants something, "do it for him." That's what Hank [Crumpton] told me. Franks is the overall commander, but the reality is Rumsfeld at the White House asserts himself over Tenet, [and] . . . that had absolutely no reflection on the ground in our decision making. None. I didn't feel it.[10]

In fact, Berntsen contends that the CIA in many ways led the war effort with support from the military:

> We are told that they [the military] are going to be there to provide close air support but nothing else. The only time that they participate with me in meetings with the Afghan [opposition] government is out of my own courtesy when I decide to bring them with me. . . . When I go in and meet with General Fahim, it's me and Fahim. When I go meet with Abdullah Abdullah, it's me and Abdullah Abdullah. When I go meet with Engineer Aref Sarwari, it's me and him. I go in and do all these meetings alone. . . . The unique part about this is that the Agency is playing a role where I'm dealing with the [Afghan] military command, I'm dealing with the equivalent of their state department [Abdullah Abdullah], and I'm dealing with the intel apparatus. I'm dealing with all of those apparatuses on my own. . . .

As far as the military goes, great guys, very very brave. Those SF teams were assigned and attached to the Agency. They were involved in keeping us alive by keeping the enemy from overrunning us. Had they not been there calling in close air support out there on the front lines, we would have been overrun. . . . But eighty percent of the meetings done with the Northern Alliance were by myself, not with them [the military].[11]

The debate over unleashing the Northern Alliance and the future of Kabul continued in the White House. At the NSC meeting on October 22, Tenet announced that they could finally release the Northern Alliance from its current stalemate with the Taliban by providing it with close air support. President Bush understood that the window of opportunity for fighting in northern Afghanistan diminished as the weather grew worse in the winter months and committed more support to the Northern Alliance. Rumsfeld expressed an alternative perspective. General Dostum at Mazar-i-Sharif had led numerous successful attacks on the Taliban front lines. But over in the Panjshir Valley and the Shomali Plains, General Fahim seemed to be waiting for American support to attack. Rumsfeld felt that no one was holding back the Northern Alliance and Fahim's idleness created the stagnation. But Rumsfeld ignored the tactical and strategic differences between the two situations. Dostum maintained a small but important island of territory to provide operational support for his fight to take one city along one short front. Fahim's coalition, on the other hand, defended almost 250 miles of front lines. Vastly outnumbered by Taliban forces, Fahim's forces sustained their efforts by controlling the high ground. If the Taliban attempted to move up into the mountains, Fahim's defensive positions could devastate the attacking forces. If Fahim's troops descended into the Shomali Plains, the Taliban's numerical advantage would result in almost certain defeat. Both sides had the manpower to defend the established front lines, but neither possessed enough of an advantage for a successful attack. Despite Triple Nickel's efforts to laser-mark targets along the front lines, American air support did little to change the war front because of its limited scope and its focus on bombing strategic targets. Indeed, the American military had refrained from shifting resources to the front lines.[12]

Confidence in the strategy plummeted within the president's cabinet over the next three days as a result of the strategic void. On October 23, Rumsfeld began developing contingency plans to deploy fifty-five thousand U.S. troops into Afghanistan. Meanwhile, satellite reconnaissance showed that the number of Taliban troops along the front lines with Fahim's Northern Alliance had doubled. Berntsen acknowledged that "the way that they were pouring across the border was [stunning]. . . . Every jihadist wannabe in Pakistan was on his way to Afghanistan to participate in the next newest jihad against the Americans."[13] In sharp contrast to the CIA's predictions, the Defense Intelligence Agency (DIA) had just released a pessimistic report asserting that the Northern Alliance would not take Mazar-i-Sharif or Kabul by winter, and "No viable Pashtun alternative exists to (the) Taliban."[14]

On October 25, National Security Advisor Condoleezza Rice met privately with the president to address the situation and relay the principals' concerns. This was a critical moment in the war. Rice considered her role as national security advisor to be the neutral chair of the principals committee meetings. "My job was to organize the decision-making process for the president, not to impose my own views, but there were times when I needed to speak up myself, and this was one of them," Rice recalled.[15] Rice asked Bush about his confidence level and contingency plans. Bush professed concern about the slow tempo, but he also put it into perspective: only five full days had passed since the first ODAs arrived in Afghanistan, and 9/11 had occurred less than fifty days earlier. Ultimately, the president conveyed confidence in the current strategy. At the NSC meeting on October 26, he asked his war cabinet to confirm that they had agreed on this strategy. Nobody wanted to contradict the president, and none of the principals voiced their concerns.[16]

Back in Afghanistan a nightmare developed for the CIA. Along with Hamid Karzai, Abdul Haq represented one of America's few Pashtun allies. At the encouragement of two American businessmen and former national security advisor Robert McFarlane, Haq and a small cadre of followers entered Afghanistan from Pakistan on October 26. Despite not holding a formal position in the U.S. government since resigning for his role in the Iran-Contra Affair, McFarlane assured Haq that the CIA would assist him. But the CIA informed Haq otherwise. Gary Berntsen was one of two CIA officers in the room when Haq called the Agency before entering Afghanistan. The CIA instructed Haq, "Do not cross that border alone. Do not cross that border without assistance or you could be captured and killed. Do not do it. We used fairly strong language with this guy . . . [but] he goes anyway."[17] Soon after, Gary Schroen received a FLASH priority cable, the most urgent alert level in the U.S. government. Taliban forces were pursuing Haq near Jalalabad. Schroen mobilized the only resource available to help Haq: a Predator drone armed with two Hellfire missiles. But the intervention proved useless. The Taliban captured Haq and proceeded to torture and execute him and his retinue. Haq's recklessness cost him his life, and America lost one of its precious few Pashtun partners in southern Afghanistan.[18]

On October 31, Gen. Tommy Franks flew to Dushanbe, Tajikistan, in his C-17 transport plane for a meeting with the key figures operating in Afghanistan. General Fahim of the Northern Alliance, Gary Schroen, Gary Berntsen, the chief of CENTCOM's Special Operations Command (SOCCENT) Rear Admiral Bert Calland, and deputy director of the CTC Hank Crumpton attended the meeting. An aggressive operations officer with years of experience in the region, Berntsen would replace Schroen as the CIA's top field commander in Afghanistan on November 4. Like his predecessor, Berntsen had received the same theatrical performance and orders about bin Laden's head in a box from Cofer Black. Franks's and Fahim's expectations generated friction at the meeting. Discouraged by Fahim's lack of action, Franks wanted to confirm that Fahim represented a reliable and functional ally. For his part, Fahim wanted assurance that the United States remained committed to supporting the Northern Alliance after three weeks of meager bombings. When Fahim requested a large monthly payment in addition to the current flow of cash, Franks muttered "bullshit" and walked out. Crumpton and Berntsen chastised Fahim for his negotiation tactics until Franks returned. The meeting marked a turning point for the campaign as the military finally committed to shift the air campaign to focus more fully on the Taliban front lines. But neither faction left the meeting feeling particularly confident in its partner's commitment.[19]

The debate in the White House over Kabul occurred at the expense of developing a cogent strategy for southern Afghanistan. Deputy Secretary of State Richard Armitage believed that there was never a coherent politico-military strategy for southern Afghanistan.[20] Colonel Mulholland considered strategy to be "too generous a word" for the operations in the south.[21] According to Amb. James Dobbins, "there wasn't much of a strategy in October. . . . [T]he center pin of the strategy was to support the Northern Alliance effort to overthrow the Taliban."[22] Although the United States aroused some limited anti-Taliban Pashtun resistance movements, the use of the Northern Alliance as the primary proxy for American forces inherently neglected southern Afghanistan. The force structure designed to combine precision-guided munitions and SOF with Afghan resistance movements could not apply to the south in the same manner due to the lack of indigenous allies. So instead of adopting a different military and political strategy that reflected the unique set of circumstances in southern Afghanistan, the White House disregarded the bottom half of the country and simply concentrated on the north.

Berntsen, who played a critical role in operations across Afghanistan, later reflected on the lack of a strategy for southern Afghanistan:

> When we go into this thing, we recognize that we are coming in with the Northern Alliance in these areas and that there isn't a southern strategy. The southern strategy, of course, is a belief that. . . . The Pakistanis imply to us that they are going to use their tribes in the South. That they are going to come. That they are going to execute. That they are going to unleash the tribes. They never do. That was what was being sold out of Pakistan. . . . So the southern strategy turns out to be Karzai, who makes initial contact and goes in on his own, and [Gul Agha] Sherzai, who goes in too. . . .
>
> Hank's view was we were going to have to wait for individuals that were supporters and then assess their value and then put teams with them possibly. And that's what he did. He got two teams into the South by just waiting a little bit. But talk from Pakistan and talk that we were going to have a southern strategy and the Pakistanis were going to help us . . . never materialized.[23]

When asked if the White House and the military had a strategy for southern Afghanistan, Berntsen responded, "No. Absolutely not. They had no strategy for that."[24] Indeed, Hank Crumpton was deeply skeptical of and objected to the belief that the Pakistanis could use their influence to resolve the situation in the south. He later wrote, "I knew the Pakistanis could not fix this. . . . Except for our Islamabad office and Tenet, we knew that the ISI was not the answer."[25] Nevertheless, Crumpton was overruled, leaving no strategy for southern Afghanistan except for a piecemeal approach of supporting the few anti-Taliban Pashtuns who emerged from the chaos.

Although military action had begun, it preceded the development of a policy and strategy upon which all operations must be based. The debate over the objectives continued in the White House and at the Pentagon well after the first bombs detonated on Afghan soil. President Bush received an initial document outlining the DOD's strategic thoughts and concepts for OEF on September 30, and Rumsfeld approved the strategic guidance document on October 3. The two-page memo stressed indirect action in the war's initial period and suggested taking actions outside of Afghanistan while forces built up so as to compel states to stop sponsoring terrorism. Nevertheless, this "Strategic Thoughts" document failed to identify and issue clear objectives to the military. On October 16, Under Secretary Feith sent a draft titled "U.S. Strategy in Afghanistan" to Rumsfeld, who revised it and sent it to Powell, Rice, and Tenet on October 30.[26] Although this document set clear and appropriate strategic objectives to be attained through the application of military force, its promulgation twenty-three days after the start of the air campaign and eleven days after the first SOF teams arrived in Afghanistan indicates a severe disconnect between strategy and operations.

Deputy National Security Advisor Stephen Hadley offered an alternative perspective. Hadley contended that the basic policy and strategy for Operation Enduring Freedom was established well before the start of military operations. According to him,

> The policy for dealing with al Qaeda was set in a document that came out on or about September 17. . . . There probably was an ongoing discussion about the objectives of the war because remember this was a war that was not planned and executed in our normal, deliberate fashion. This was a war thrust on us on 9/11 when our nation was attacked. So it's not really a surprise that four to six weeks into it, there may be some clarification of the second-order objectives that Rumsfeld is issuing to his commanders. . . . The first-order objectives—the kinds that were set by the president of the United States—I think were pretty clear and well understood.[27]

The pressure to respond to the September 11 terrorist attacks with military force permeated the White House, likely encouraging operations even in the absence of a coherent strategy. National Security Advisor Rice stated,

> After September 11, there was a tremendous pressure to do something, and do it soon. The president kept saying, "We are not going to rush into this." I remember him telling me, "I will feel the pulse of the American people when we have to have done something." So while some wanted to start dropping bombs on September 12, the president was very cautious. The truth of the matter is that we had to act quickly.[28]

Secretary Rumsfeld also felt the need to act. In an October 10 memo to the chairman and vice chairman of the Joint Chiefs of Staff, Rumsfeld expressed his sense of urgency: "It has been a month since the attack on the Pentagon. More people are going to be killed if we don't produce some results fast. We owe it to the country to get this accomplished and fast. If we delay longer, more Americans could be killed."[29]

Despite the belated insertion of special operations forces into Afghanistan, the strategic void limited American effectiveness. The White House leadership continued the impasse by dithering over the role of the Northern Alliance in taking Kabul. No coherent strategy emerged for southern Afghanistan. Along with personality clashes, the command structure between the CIA and the DOD complicated the situation. The absence of empirical results reduced confidence in the overall strategy, and the pressure to respond encouraged operations without a solid strategic foundation. But as the military redirected air assets to the Taliban front lines, the situation began to change. During November, city after city fell to the Northern Alliance.

6

DOMINOES

October 21 to November 27, 2001

You knock over the first one, and what will happen to the last one is the certainty that it will go over very quickly.

— PRESIDENT DWIGHT EISENHOWER[1]

The United States of America scrambled to respond to the devastating 9/11 terrorist attacks but lacked the proper intelligence, military plans, and defined objectives to act immediately. Personalities and bureaucracies clashed during the high-pressure planning process in the White House. And a strategic void over the political future of the country followed an operational impasse in getting troops into Afghanistan. However, the momentum of the war effort began to favor the United States in November 2001. Positive results finally emerged when air operations shifted from bombing strategic targets to close air support of the Northern Alliance. By mid-November, close to a dozen ODAs had entered Afghanistan, including a few teams in the south. Each incremental step in the war effort—close air support, ODAs attached to numerous resistance forces, increased CIA presence, and continued diplomatic efforts—interacted to produce the necessary power to topple the Taliban. Its rapid defeat in important cities across the country surprised the world, including the top civilian and military leadership in Washington. But as the cities fell like dominoes, the success against the Taliban overshadowed the lackluster effort to pursue specific al Qaeda cells and their leadership in Afghanistan.

While snow fell across the mountains of northern Afghanistan on October 21, B-52 and B-1 strategic bombers loitered twenty thousand feet above the

Darya Suf River, approximately fifty miles south of Mazar-i-Sharif. Standing on an overlook adjacent to the valley below, Gen. Abdul Rashid Dostum helped Capt. Mitch Nelson of ODA 595 get his first glimpse of the enemy. Or at least he thought it was the enemy. Leading the way in the first U.S. military battle of the twenty-first century, ODA 595 had trekked up the side of a mountain on horses fitted with extraordinarily unpleasant wooden saddles and stirrups sized for the much smaller Afghans. Tired, sore, and five miles away from the target, Captain Nelson found it impossible to discern what he was seeing. So the Special Forces (SF) soldier asked Dostum how he knew that the identified target was a Taliban bunker. Dostum picked up his Motorola radio, tuned it to the Taliban's channel, and said, "Come in, come in, come in. This is General Dostum. I am here with the Americans, and they have come to kill you. . . . Tell me, what is your position?"[2] The Taliban soldiers on the other end had no comprehension of U.S. military capabilities and proceeded to confirm their location to Dostum and ODA 595.[3]

Captain Nelson was not carrying a Special Operations Forces Laser Acquisition Marker (SOFLAM) that day and instead had to calculate the location of the Taliban's bunker by hand. Using a handheld GPS device and a range finder, Nelson determined his location and distance to the target. He then calculated the direction from his location to the enemy in order to create a vector from the data he compiled. Looking back and forth between his binoculars and a terrain map provided by Dostum, Nelson pinpointed the location of the enemy bunker on the map and relayed those grid coordinates to a B-52 overhead. The aircrew programmed the coordinates into a Joint Direct Attack Munition (JDAM) bomb and released it from the weapons bay. Commonly referred to as a type of "smart bomb," JDAMs are state-of-the-art tail kits that, for about $20,000 per bomb, convert obsolete "dumb bombs" into GPS-guided weapons of extreme precision. JDAMs dropped anywhere within a fifteen-mile radius use their internal GPS systems to guide themselves within five meters of the programmed target. Thirty seconds later, Dostum and Nelson watched as a mushroom cloud rose in the valley below them.[4]

Unfortunately, the bomb landed a mile off target. Nelson had known that five miles was too far to accurately pinpoint targets without a SOFLAM, but Dostum had insisted that they could not safely get closer, so the SF captain gave it a shot. The second bomb missed by the same amount. The third bomb got within two hundred yards of the Taliban bunker, but the fourth and fifth landed two miles away. Frustrated, Nelson called off the sixth attempt. Dostum, however, was elated. He tuned his radio to the Taliban frequency and bragged about how, with the help of the Americans, he made explosions rain from the sky. Nelson knew he could do better, and soon he would have his chance.[5]

Abdul Rashid Dostum lay at the center of U.S. efforts to capture the strategic city of Mazar-i-Sharif. He was the quintessential Afghan warlord. As an ethnic Uzbek born in northern Afghanistan, Dostum spent ten years fighting for the Soviets in Afghanistan after joining the Afghan Army in 1978. Dostum continued to support the communist Afghan government under President Najibullah.[6] However, according to Pakistani journalist Ahmed Rashid,

> In 1992 Dostum was the first to rebel against his mentor Najibullah, thereby establishing his reputation for treachery and political opportunism. The hard-drinking Dostum then became a "good Muslim." Since then, he had, at one time or another, allied himself with everyone—Masud [Ahmed Shah Massoud], Hikmatyar [Gulbuddin Hekmatyar], the Taliban, Masud again—and betrayed everyone with undisguised aplomb. He had also been on every country's payroll receiving funds from Russia, Uzbekistan, Iran, Pakistan and lately Turkey. . . . If there was one consistent trait, it was his deep opposition to the extremist fundamentalism of Pashtun factions, even before the advent of the Taliban.[7]

Dostum was as ruthless as he was opportunistic. When Ahmed Rashid first met Dostum, he arrived to find the courtyard bloody and scattered with bits of flesh. Upon inquiry, Rashid discovered that Dostum had ordered one of his soldiers who was caught stealing to be tied to the treads of a Soviet tank and instructed the rest of his troops to watch as the tank drove around the courtyard, grinding the soldier into pieces.[8] Nonetheless, Dostum was a formidable opponent of the Taliban and therefore gained the support of the United States.

On October 22, the day after the ineffective bombing runs, Dostum led his forces and part of ODA 595 on a four-hour horse ride in order to get closer to Taliban positions. Now only two miles away, Captain Nelson could clearly see the Taliban's bunkers, tanks, and antiaircraft turrets. While Nelson acquired targets, Dostum organized three hundred of his troops into two waves of cavalry raids. As Dostum's forces began the one-mile charge, Nelson delivered direct hits onto Taliban strongholds. Tanks and fortifications exploded as the cavalrymen raced from ridge to ridge, dodging Taliban bullets, returning fire, and exchanging rocket-propelled grenades. Just as victory appeared likely, a Taliban tank and armored infantry vehicle arrived in the distance and opened fire on Dostum's troops. Nelson radioed for aerial support, but the pilot overhead was running out of fuel and unable to help. As the sun set, Dostum's forces turned around and retreated, giving up the territory for which they had fought. Although not yet a full deployment of U.S. aerial resources, the attack represented a substantial improvement from the previous weeks of stagnation. Signals intercepts over the following days indicated panic as Taliban commanders sent hundreds of reinforcements from Mazar-i-Sharif to the front lines.[9] The small but concerted attack revealed the weakness of the Taliban forces.

On October 23, Dostum invited Captain Nelson and part of ODA 595, CIA officer Mike Spann, and two other Agency officers to participate in a cavalry raid. Captain Nelson directed bombs onto Taliban positions just as the first wave of Dostum's cavalry arrived within shooting distance of the enemy. As the Americans followed the assault, themselves on horseback, a Taliban soldier who survived the first wave took aim at Spann. Spann raised his AK-47 and shot the Taliban soldier in the head. When Dostum's forces arrived at the final ridge separating themselves from the enemy, they became trapped by gunfire. Dostum ordered his men to continue but they had frozen in fear. Furious, Dostum stepped off of his horse, grabbed some additional clips for his AK-47, and charged the Taliban front line by himself, firing wildly at the enemy. Inspired by their commander's bravado or embarrassed by their own cowardly actions, Dostum's men followed. The remaining Taliban soldiers abandoned their positions, retreating or surrendering to Dostum's forces.[10] And so it was that the United States and the Afghan opposition won their first battle.

Dostum was making substantial progress on the Mazar-i-Sharif front with the support of the CIA team, codenamed team "Alpha," and ODA 595. But over the last week of October and the first week of November, a disconnect grew between the White House and the reality of the situation in Afghanistan. At an

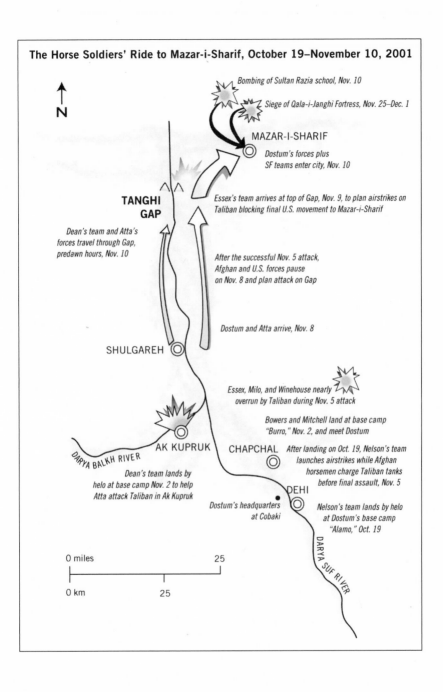

The Horse Soldiers' Ride to Mazar-i-Sharif, October 19–November 10, 2001

N

Bombing of Sultan Razia school, Nov. 10

Siege of Qala-i-Janghi Fortress, Nov. 25–Dec. 1

MAZAR-I-SHARIF

Dostum's forces plus
SF teams enter city, Nov. 10

TANGHI
GAP

Essex's team arrives at top of Gap, Nov. 9, to plan airstrikes on
Taliban blocking final U.S. movement to Mazar-i-Sharif

Dean's team and Atta's
forces travel through Gap,
predawn hours, Nov. 10

After the successful Nov. 5 attack,
Afghan and U.S. forces pause
on Nov. 8 and plan attack on Gap

Dostum and Atta arrive, Nov. 8

SHULGAREH

Essex, Milo, and Winehouse nearly
overrun by Taliban during Nov. 5 attack

Bowers and Mitchell land at base camp
"Burro," Nov. 2, and meet Dostum

AK KUPRUK

CHAPCHAL

After landing on Oct. 19, Nelson's team
launches airstrikes while Afghan
horsemen charge Taliban tanks
before final assault, Nov. 5

DARYA BALKH RIVER

Dean's team lands by
helo at base camp Nov. 2 to help
Atta attack Taliban in Ak Kupruk

DEHI

Dostum's headquarters
at Cobaki

Nelson's team lands by helo
at Dostum's base camp
"Alamo," Oct. 19

0 miles   25

0 km   25

DARYA SUF RIVER

NSC meeting on November 2 to discuss the war's progress, the principals expressed frustration over the still static situation. Franks provided a dim assessment of Fahim, and Cheney suggested further developing the contingency plans for fifty-five thousand troops. Bush directed Franks to continue with those efforts.[11] Under Secretary of Defense Doug Feith later described the situation:

> Once we got the A-Teams in, the major question was how to spur the Afghans to fight. There was a hope that the shift towards close air support from the United States would induce action, but it seemed to take forever. The political criticism generated in the "quagmire debate" added to this pressure. . . .
>
> If we were going to have the shock effect that we desired on state sponsors of terrorism, it was very important that the United States not look ineffectual or impotent. That was a big strategic fear, and it argued for inducing the Northern Alliance to start capturing ground immediately, and not after the winter of 2001/2002 was behind us.[12]

Nonetheless, the principals viewed the shift of air assets toward the Northern Alliance as a minor detail, not a game-changer, and had confused the lag between the beginning of close air support and tangible results with a continuation of the strategic and operational impasses.

And despite the progress that Captain Nelson was making on the battlefield, he was receiving messages from his superiors that demonstrated this disconnect. In response to one particularly rash query, Nelson wrote what would become one of the most famous dispatches of the campaign:

> I am advising a man on how to best employ light infantry and horse cavalry in the attack against Taliban T-55s [tanks], mortars, artillery, personnel carriers, and machine guns—a tactic which I think became outdated with the invention of the Gatling gun. [They] have done this every day we have been on the ground. They have attacked with 10 rounds of ammunition per man, with snipers having less than 100 rounds—little water and less food. I have observed a PK gunner who walked 10-plus miles to get to the fight, who was proud to show me his artificial right leg from the knee down.

We have witnessed the horse cavalry bounding overwatch from spur to spur to attack Taliban strongpoints—the last several kilometers under mortar, artillery, and sniper fire. There is little medical care if injured, only a donkey ride to the aid station, which is a dirt hut.

We could not do what we are doing without the close air support—everywhere I go the civilian and *mujahideen* soldiers are always telling me they are glad the U.S.A. has come. They all speak of their hopes for a better Afghanistan once the Taliban are gone.[13]

Day after day, the Taliban ceded miles of territory to Dostum's forces. ODA 595 would use the SOFLAM to direct laser-guided bombs onto targets while Dostum's troops followed up with cavalry raids. On November 4, ODA 534 inserted to join Gen. Mohammed Atta, a second warlord supporting the efforts to capture Mazar-i-Sharif.[14] On November 5, Deputy Secretary of Defense Paul Wolfowitz told the war cabinet that the military directed 90 percent of the day's sorties for close air support of anti-Taliban opposition forces. That day, two BLU-82 Daisy Cutters—fifteen-thousand-pound bombs the size of a small car that were originally designed to create eight-hundred-foot helicopter landing zones in the dense jungles of Vietnam—were dropped onto Taliban positions outside of Mazar-i-Sharif. Dostum followed the destruction with a cavalry raid as Atta's force flanked the Taliban, causing them to retreat. But at a press briefing on November 6, Rumsfeld claimed that it would take months to defeat the Taliban and al Qaeda. The principals at the White House still did not notice the progress from the operational shift.[15]

Moving north along the valley created by the Darya Suf River, Dostum's and Atta's forces arrived on November 9 at the last major obstacle in their offensive for Mazar-i-Sharif. The Tangi Gap is a small opening in the lateral mountain range and the only viable northerly approach to Mazar-i-Sharif. Fifteen miles of flat plains separated the Tangi Gap from the city, and the Taliban had chosen this location to make their final stand. Dozens of Taliban rockets landed just as the Afghans and Americans entered the canyon. Those who made it through the Gap were confronted with sheets of bullets from Taliban small-arms fire. As ODA 595 and ODA 534 laser-marked targets along the front lines, Franks focused the day's ordnance—90 to 120 sorties—on Mazar-i-Sharif. After a two-hour firefight, Dostum's and Atta's forces succeeded in clearing the Tangi

Gap. The path finally lay clear for U.S. and opposition forces to take the strategic city.[16]

Mazar-i-Sharif fell to Northern Alliance generals Abdul Rashid Dostum and Mohammed Atta on November 10. Just a day earlier, Tenet had told a doubtful group at the White House that Northern Alliance forces might capture Mazar-i-Sharif in the next forty-eight hours. When the Taliban defenses crumbled, Dostum's and Atta's soldiers pushed northward into the city. Celebrations erupted as the people of Mazar-i-Sharif received Dostum as a liberator and hero. Franks had not anticipated that the city would fall so quickly; rather, he only predicted a favorable military situation by the end of November. The news surprised Rice, and Rumsfeld did not even believe that the city had fallen.[17] Despite little strategic guidance and substantial pessimism at the White House, the battle for Mazar-i-Sharif established a model for the war in Afghanistan: joint interagency teams attached to resistance factions and backed by close air support to liberate Taliban-controlled cities in a matter of days.

Underpinning the success at Mazar-i-Sharif was the process that Cofer Black and Hank Crumpton had devised for executing the war in Afghanistan. After 9/11, the CIA had created a new office within the Counterterrorism Center entitled Special Operations (CTC/SO) to manage Agency operations in Afghanistan. Unlike the rigidity and hierarchy of the military, the CIA established a flat command structure to enable maximum flexibility in its operations. Instead of the segmented, cubicle-and-office layout characteristic of U.S. government buildings, CTC/SO was based in one large room with approximately sixty workstations face-to-face on one long table. At one end of the table was a targeting cell designed to exploit the intelligence collected at CTC/SO and coordinate attacks with CENTCOM.[18] CIA field commander Gary Berntsen, who reported to CTC/SO, described the setup:

They [Hank and Cofer] gave us the maximum flexibility. Hank set the table for all the team leaders to act independently.

Normally, in a normal conflict . . . you have one guy—Gary Schroen was out there originally—and here is Gary Schroen. He's an SIS-3, a senior intelligence service officer grade 3, and he is [the equivalent of] a three-star general. And so, the way that the agency runs is that you send a guy out there that is in charge of the whole country.

Schroen is turning sixty, so he had to be removed. But the other reason to remove him is [that] by removing him, Hank, who is an SIS-2, outranks all of us [field officers]. And so he sits me down and says, "Schroen was in this position before. You are not going to be. I want you to run your sector of the country, which is huge. You can have multiple battlefields, but let me handle these other pieces. Let us run from technology. We can do this." I was like, "No problem, Hank. However you want to do this." When Schroen is there, he's rightfully considered the chief of the whole place. When I enter, and the other teams enter, then it is cut into segments. . . .

So for the first time, we don't have a senior officer in the country who is responsible for managing that [war effort]. [Instead,] we have multiple teams being commanded by a headquarters component. We did that for that element there, and I don't think we've done it ever since. . . .

It's taking intelligence and being able to immediately respond without running up the chain, without asking for permission. Right now, the military can't go off a base without writing an op [operations] order and having it approved up nine levels. Then I just made the decision to proceed. It was a very flat chain of command. So we would make decisions right on the spot based on the intelligence that we had at hand. That was the system that Hank designed. . . .

Hank set up a plan that allowed such rapid action that it was difficult for anyone to keep track. The Taliban couldn't keep track, and it was difficult for the U.S. government to keep track because we were allowed to move that fast. It was a great plan for victory [but] hard for everyone else to keep up. . . . We didn't ask permission on really major events. I won't say that Hank was running this out of his pocket—he understood what was going on. He was the focal point in Washington, D.C.[19]

Osama bin Laden and his deputy, Ayman al-Zawahiri, attended the funeral of Juma Khan Namangani, the founder of the Islamic Movement of Uzbekistan, in Kabul the day before Mazar-i-Sharif fell. Afterward, they met with Pakistani journalist Hamid Mir for an interview. Sitting next to the

Kalashnikov AK-74 he took from a Soviet soldier at the Battle of Jaji, bin Laden defended the 9/11 attacks, although he still did not take responsibility. In a bluff, he told Mir that al Qaeda possessed weapons of mass destruction to deter an American WMD attack. Sometime over the next five days, bin Laden and Zawahiri traveled to Jalalabad.[20] Clearly, the American war effort had done little to restrict bin Laden's movements around Kabul and eastern Afghanistan.

By November 11, nearly a dozen ODA teams operated across northern Afghanistan alongside with Northern Alliance commanders, allowing the strategy to unfold rapidly. ODA 585 inserted near Kunduz on October 23 to support Burillah Khan. ODA 553 attached to Hazara commander Kareem Khahlili in Bamiyan on November 2. On November 4, ODA 534 inserted near Mazar-i-Sharif to support Gen. Mohammed Atta. In the Panjshir Valley, ODA 594 arrived on November 9 to support Fahim as Triple Nickel (ODA 555) moved to Bagram Air Base near Kabul. The same day, ODA 586 attached to Gen. Daoud Khan in Kunduz. On November 11, ODA 554 deployed to Herat to support Ismail Khan. After the fall of Mazar-i-Sharif, Northern Alliance forces moved northeast, trapping the Taliban in Kunduz as Russian troops secretly deployed to the Tajikistan border to block the only escape route. Taloqan and Bamiyan fell on the 11th, along with Herat the next day.[21] The events in Afghanistan outpaced the understanding of the principals in Washington, and nobody was prepared for what would happen next.

On November 12, Northern Alliance commander Bismullah Khan led his forces across the Shomali Plains, reaching the outskirts of Kabul as Taliban forces retreated from the city. Just the day before, twenty-five air strikes cleared the way for an assault on Kabul by killing roughly two thousand Taliban and destroying twenty-nine tanks and six command posts. Although the American leadership instructed Khan to stop outside of Kabul and wait for UN troops to arrive and stabilize the capital, the ultimate treasure lay within the commander's grasp. The situation progressed so quickly that few could stop the momentum. Citing reports of disorder, Khan entered Kabul with two thousand troops to provide security and stability. Pashtun commander Abdurrab Rasul Sayyaf approached from the south and joined Bismullah Khan by deploying five hundred fighters to Kabul. Thirteen days after air assets had been redirected to focus on close air support, the Northern Alliance controlled half of Afghanistan and had allied with Pashtun factions to occupy Kabul. President

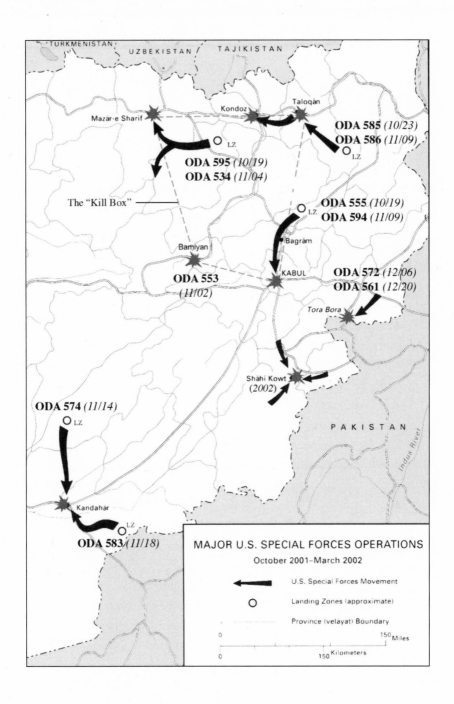

ODA 585 *(10/23)*
ODA 586 *(11/09)*

ODA 595 *(10/19)*
ODA 534 *(11/04)*

The "Kill Box"

ODA 555 *(10/19)*
ODA 594 *(11/09)*

ODA 553
(11/02)

ODA 572 *(12/06)*
ODA 561 *(12/20)*

Shāhi Kowt
(2002)

ODA 574 *(11/14)*

ODA 583 *(11/18)*

MAJOR U.S. SPECIAL FORCES OPERATIONS
October 2001–March 2002

U.S. Special Forces Movement

Landing Zones (approximate)

Province (velayat) Boundary

0   150 Miles

0   150 Kilometers

73

Bush summarized the war cabinet's reaction to the events: "It's amazing how fast the situation has changed. It is a stunner, isn't it?"[22]

The principals had devised the policy of stopping the Northern Alliance outside of Kabul and sending UN troops to patrol and stabilize the city in order to prevent alienating the Pashtuns in southern Afghanistan. Some were concerned that the Pashtun plurality would perceive the occupation of Kabul by the Northern Alliance as American support for Tajik and Uzbek domination. Rumsfeld, however, disagreed with the policy of stopping short.[23] Deputy CIA Director John McLaughlin also opposed the policy:

> One of the arguments that ensued when Kabul fell so quickly was, can we encourage the Northern Alliance to move into Kabul and essentially establish order? One school of thought was we have to worry about that because they may fall back to persecution of their tribal competitors. At CIA, and I personally argued, no, we have to let them go in there and do this because that's what we told them we are going to do. And if we don't let them go in and basically take over in Kabul for this period of time, we are going to lose all of our credibility because we have come into Afghanistan and said that we want to get rid of that government in Kabul. And bingo, we have. And now, if we try to hold them back out of some fear of what they might do or how they might behave, it would destroy our credibility with them.[24]

On the ground in Afghanistan, the U.S. policy of stopping short did not affect the actions of the Northern Alliance. Gary Berntsen later recalled the chaos and excitement that surrounded the fall of Kabul:

> The White House assumed that the Northern Alliance would stop five miles outside the city. None of us believed that. In our hearts, I was thrilled when they went through. We were celebrating when they blew right through that. We wanted to stay five miles outside while the Taliban was still in that damn city? We want to stop short? How are we going to pursue? It made absolutely no sense. . . .
>
> The Northern Alliance didn't butcher people in the city. I knew from my discussions that they weren't going to do that. I didn't give

them the wink to go in. I did say, "Look, this is the policy here." But we were sitting around and said, "Are they going to stop? No way!" . . .

When we went into the city, the DDO [deputy director of operations], Jim Pavitt, was panicked. . . . It was only when the director told him it was okay that he didn't get upset.[25]

At the NSC meeting on November 13, the principals discussed how to handle the day's events and unknowingly set the stage for the biggest failure of the war. The Bush administration's plan called for a multilateral force backed by UN mandate to occupy Kabul and provide security until the various factions agreed to a sustainable political solution. Bush said, "US forces will not stay. . . . We've got a job to do with al Qaeda. We need to look at WMD targets."[26] When Rice inquired about Pakistan, Rumsfeld said, "Tommy [Franks] says the first priority is to close the border. Our concept is to—," at which point President Bush interrupted him, saying, "If he [Osama bin Laden] moves elsewhere, we're just going to get him there."[27] The president's focus on WMD targets and his disregard for securing the Pakistan border established priorities that would result in the one of the most important and consequential failures of the global war on terrorism.

November 14 proved just as eventful as the day before. With most of the northern cities under Northern Alliance control, the CIA and the military began to focus on operations in the south and east. Gary Berntsen had intended to insert a team 115 miles east of Kabul in Asadabad, a rural town in the lawless Pech Valley of Kunar Province on the border with Pakistan.[28] Kunar was a common thoroughfare for insurgents traveling between Afghanistan and Pakistan and represented some of the most hostile territory in the region. From Asadabad, the team would fight its way southward along the Afghanistan-Pakistan border to cover the eastern exit from Kabul and Jalalabad. However, the developing situation necessitated an alternative deployment. The Taliban capital of Kandahar represented the biggest challenge but also the biggest reward if captured. To the north of Kandahar, Hamid Karzai and his cadre entered the town of Tarin Kowt along with three special operations soldiers, ODA 574, and the six intelligence officers who were initially assigned to Asadabad. Around the same time, a U.S. air strike in Kabul killed Mohammed Atef, al Qaeda's top military commander.[29]

Meanwhile, Pashtun commander Abdurrab Rasul Sayyaf, who only a day earlier occupied Kabul, moved his troops due east to Jalalabad. Backed by close air support, Sayyaf and a couple other Pashtun resistance forces launched an assault on the city, causing the Taliban to flee and creating a localized power vacuum that lasted for a week. The offensive barely missed bin Laden, who arrived at Tora Bora from Jalalabad at roughly the same time that Jalalabad fell.[30]

Behind the mayhem in eastern Afghanistan, a CIA pursuit team surreptitiously entered Jalalabad to go after al Qaeda deputy Ayman al-Zawahiri. The CIA had tracked Zawahiri to a hospital in Jalalabad and was preparing to assault his location when the city fell. The ensuing chaos, however, allowed Zawahiri to escape before the Agency team could act. According to Gary Berntsen, "I was most close to getting him [Zawahiri] . . . [but in the end] he eluded us."[31]

An undertone of irony persisted in Abdurrab Rasul Sayyaf's pursuit of Osama bin Laden. Sayyaf was a notorious Afghan Islamist and Wahhabist who had supported bin Laden when he arrived in Afghanistan in 1996.[32] Some sources indicate that Sayyaf was a mentor of bin Laden and encouraged him to bring Arabs into the Soviet jihad. Sayyaf had a documented history of human rights violations and massacres. And thousands of miles away, according to some sources, the Filipino terrorist organization Abu Sayyaf was named after him. But despite his religious fervor, Sayyaf was an ardent opponent of the Taliban and therefore joined the Northern Alliance.[33] Although Sayyaf was part of the Northern Alliance, he had—knowingly or otherwise—vouched for the two al Qaeda operatives who assassinated Massoud on September 9, 2001.[34] Now, five years after Sayyaf welcomed bin Laden to Afghanistan, he was engaged in a war against his former protégé.

The inhabitants of Tarin Kowt rebelled against the Taliban and killed the local Taliban mayor on November 16. Hamid Karzai and ODA 574 saw the uprising as a promising opportunity to take the town. As resistance forces arrived on its outskirts, intelligence detected a Taliban convoy of one hundred vehicles with up to one thousand Taliban reinforcements traveling from Kandahar to reestablish control of the strategic northerly passage to Kandahar. Close to fifty Pashtun fighters joined ODA 574 in establishing defensive positions overlooking a bottleneck in the valley that contained the entrance from

Kandahar. With dedicated air support, ODA 574 guided numerous bombs onto the convoy as Taliban forces attempted to pass the choke point. But despite the tactical advantage, the Pashtun fighters retreated and ODA 574 was forced to follow. Later that evening, ODA 574 established defensive positions at another location and directed air support to destroy thirty trucks in the convoy, killing three hundred Taliban.[35] Although the battle succeeded in repelling Taliban reinforcements and taking Tarin Kowt, the reliance on a ragtag and flighty group of Pashtun resistance forces dampened the effectiveness of the ambush.

With most of the northern Afghan cities under Northern Alliance control, the military focus shifted to southern Afghanistan. While Karzai and ODA 574 approached Kandahar from the north, ODA 583 inserted with Gul Agha Sherzai at Shin Narai to approach the Taliban capital from the southeast. November 22 marked the introduction of conventional troops when two Marine Corps infantry battalions led by Brig. Gen. James Mattis arrived at Camp Rhino, the same landing strip near Kandahar captured on October 19 by Army Rangers. That same day, ODA 583 and eight hundred of Sherzai's troops departed toward Kandahar along Highway 4. After a short battle at Takht-e Pol on November 24, Sherzai's forces arrived within viewing distance of the Kandahar Airport, and ODA 583 guided air strikes onto Taliban positions continuously for seven days. The Kandahar offensive now depended on Karzai's progress as he approached from the north.[36]

The Northern Alliance's rapid eastward offensive from Mazar-i-Sharif to Taloqan sequestered Taliban fighters in the north, causing thousands of them—including approximately a thousand foreign militants—to retreat into the city of Kunduz to make a final stand. During the two weeks of fierce fighting between the Northern Alliance and besieged Taliban and al Qaeda troops, the ISI embarked on a furtive operation to evacuate hundreds of Pakistani agents and Frontier Corps soldiers still supporting Taliban units in Kunduz. One senior intelligence analyst claimed,

The request was made by Musharraf to Bush, but Cheney took charge—a token of who was handling Musharraf at the time. The approval was not shared with anyone at State . . . until well after the event. Musharraf said Pakistan needed to save its dignity and its valued people. Two planes were involved, which made several sorties a night over several nights. They took off from air bases in Chitral and Gilgit in Pakistan's northern areas, and landed in Kunduz, where the evacuees were waiting on the tarmac. Certainly hundreds and perhaps as many as one thousand people escaped. Hundreds of ISI officers, Taliban commanders, and foot soldiers belonging to the IMU [Islamic Movement of Uzbekistan] and al Qaeda personnel boarded the planes. What was sold as a minor extraction turned into a major air bridge. The frustrated U.S. SOF who watched it from the surrounding high ground dubbed it "Operation Evil Airlift."[37]

U.S. intelligence analysts, diplomats, ambassadors, journalists, and members of the International Committee of the Red Cross and the United Nations have confirmed that the Kunduz airlift occurred in mid-November 2001. On November 24, 2001, the director general of Pakistan's Inter-Services Public Relations Directorate, Maj. Gen. Rashid Qureshi, stated that the Pakistani government was pursuing negotiations with the United States in order to evacuate Pakistanis from Kunduz. Indian intelligence quickly detected the evacuation flights and ultimately concluded that up to five thousand Pakistanis, Taliban, and foreign militants were "rescued" during the operation. While the Indian assessment is likely exaggerated, estimates of the number of enemy forces at Kunduz indicate that thousands of militants were unaccounted for at the conclusion of the battle.[38]

Gary Berntsen, the top CIA officer in Afghanistan at the time of the Kunduz airlift, was not informed of the operation. With piercing fury in his eyes, Berntsen recalled how the Kunduz airlift unfolded:

My understanding is that Musharraf called the president, said many of Pakistan's favorite sons are trapped up in Kunduz, they were monitoring the Taliban, they need to be flown out. And so the U.S. military opened an air corridor—they had to have, we controlled the skies—and flew planes in and landed and evacuated several plane-loads of these guys. . . . Amrullah Saleh comes in screaming at me, "Why are you Americans trying to save the Taliban?" . . . I got in a screaming match with him. He explained to me in detail [what had happened]. . . . I got in a vehicle, and I drove immediately to see General Dailey. He denied it.

When I left, I didn't believe him. . . . I knew at that point that the U.S. military had opened up an air corridor to evacuate the Pakistanis. And I thought to myself, how in the world could this be happening? How could they have been so snookered as to do this? It was just plane after plane. Maybe two or three planeloads of guys. And the Taliban guys all fought their way on the plane. The leadership of the Taliban. . . . were evacuated from the north. The Northern Alliance was just ballistic, and they felt completely betrayed by us. And I don't blame them. I felt betrayed. . . .

Only the White House could have authorized that. . . . [It was] the height of stupidity. Men fighting these guys on the ground, and you're evacuating them, and our sons have been fighting these guys. The most irresponsible and foolish act of the war. I can understand the issue of Tora Bora. . . . There is absolutely no excuse for what happened in Kunduz. Absolutely none. . . .

Why not have them surrender to U.S. forces? Turn yourself in, and if you're Pakistani we'll take you out. Simple. Pretty easy. Just show up, here's the grid coordinate. Get there. . . . But to allow them to fly planes in like that. . . . To tell you that I was apoplectic was an understatement.[39]

The Kunduz airlift was kept so secret that even Secretary of State Colin Powell was not informed.[40] While Under Secretary of Defense Doug Feith was also unaware of the airlift, he explained the context that may have enabled it to occur. "I don't know anything about the Kunduz airlift," Feith recalled. "If Musharraf called the president, it would not surprise me at all that the president would tell Condi or Rumsfeld about the call. Rumsfeld would have been receptive in general to help Musharraf. Rumsfeld considered him to be an important partner for the U.S. military."[41]

Although it is clear that some al Qaeda and Taliban operatives escaped Kunduz on Pakistani planes, the quantity and identities of those militants remain a mystery. The Kunduz airlift nevertheless clearly illustrated the level of integration of the ISI, the Taliban, and possibly al Qaeda that immediately followed 9/11. Although these connections were ostensibly severed following Musharraf's acceptance of the seven American demands, the legacies of the previous decade proved difficult to undo. According to Dexter Filkins, the journalist who wrote the first article exposing the Kunduz airlift, "there was no question that Pakistani airplanes were coming in. . . . The Pakistanis had a lot of military advisors in there, and it sounds like they all got off, and lots of other people got on the planes too."[42] Seymour Hersh later reported:

> The airlift "made sense at the time," the C.I.A. analyst said. "Many of the people they spirited away were the Taliban leadership"—who Pakistan hoped could play a role in a postwar Afghan government. According to this person, "Musharraf wanted to have these people to put another card on the table" in future political negotiations. "We were supposed to have access to them," he said, but "it didn't happen," and the rescued Taliban remain unavailable to American intelligence.[43]

The Northern Alliance controlled all of northern Afghanistan by the end of November. The Taliban had lost its last stronghold in the north with the fall of Kunduz on November 24. Meanwhile, General Dostum negotiated the surrender of about three hundred al Qaeda fighters and transferred them to a makeshift prison at Qala-i-Jangi, an eighteenth-century fortress on the outskirts of Mazar-i-Sharif, where CIA operatives would interrogate them. But Dostum's forces did not search the detainees, who concealed weapons and explosives underneath their clothing. The prisoners rioted on November 25, taking control of part of the fortress and killing CIA officer Mike Spann, the first American combat casualty in Afghanistan. After four days of heavy bombardments, the remaining al Qaeda prisoners surrendered when Dostum's forces flooded their basement shelter with cold water.[44] Journalist Ahmed Rashid reported that Dostum refused to make similar mistakes with prisoners again:

> Several thousand surviving Taliban prisoners [under Dostum's control] were packed into container lorries—stuffed in like sardines, 250 or more to a container—so that the prisoners' knees were against their chests and there was no air to breathe save for holes punched through by machine-gun bullets. The prisoners were driven to a jail in Dostum's

home town of Shiberghan. Only a handful of people in each of the thirty containers survived the journey—in one container only 6 out of 220 survived, according to UN officials. The dead were taken out to the Dasht-e-Leili desert and buried in huge pits dug by a bulldozer.[45]

Soon after the death of Mike Spann at Qala-i-Jangi, Berntsen received a cable from CIA headquarters that banned Agency officers from entering prisons in Afghanistan.[46] Berntsen read the message to his subordinates and proceeded to tear it up. He instructed his team:

Go back into the prisons tomorrow. I don't care what the director [of Central Intelligence] says. If he wants to be in charge, he can come out here. And we kept going. And that's how we found out what the next bombing was going to be. The Singapore attack. So I disregarded those specific orders given to me by headquarters because I thought they were stupid. I knew they were from the seventh floor. I assumed that's why Hank sent me. . . . We lost Spann [and it was] heartbreaking. But it's war. It's going to happen.[47]

The handling of high-value prisoners proved to be another stumbling block for U.S. forces in Afghanistan even before the establishment of Guantanamo Bay detention facility. According to Berntsen,

We captured some high-value targets. Immediately, I tried to turn them over to the military. They didn't want them. And we had to fight with them to get them to take the prisoners. I mean, I literally had to make phone calls back there and had to threaten to fly them [the prisoners] to a third country and turn them over to that country. So that's what I did. I threatened to fly them on a plane up to a third country because they had been conducting hostile acts against that country, and I figured let them talk to them. Because I didn't want agency officers interviewing them. I did not want that. I forbade my men from interrogating them.[48]

The complications that Berntsen faced in handling high-value detainees was a harbinger of what was to come in the ensuing years of the war.

Meanwhile, the Bonn Conference, a UN summit to establish an agreement on the political future of Afghanistan, began on November 27, 2001. President Bush appointed Amb. James Dobbins, a seasoned diplomat at the State Department, as America's special envoy to the Afghan opposition. Dobbins's criteria for a new Afghan government were "an Afghan government that would replace the Taliban's, unite the opposition, secure international support, cooperate in hunting down al Qaeda's remnants, and relieve the United States of the need to occupy and run the country."[49] In its final form on December 5, the Bonn Agreement established the Afghan Interim Authority (AIA) and chose Hamid Karzai to lead the transitional government for the next six months. Afterward a *loya jirga* (traditional Afghan grand assembly) would convene to choose a replacement for Karzai, write a national constitution, and arrange for national elections.[50]

The operational and strategic stalemate of October broke during November, resulting in the rapid defeat of the Taliban across the north of the country. The surge of special operations forces and CIA operatives into Afghanistan, combined with the shift from bombing strategic targets to close air support, had provided the Northern Alliance with the necessary advantage to destroy the Taliban and drive them from the northern cities. Despite the CSAR conundrum, the military engaged in risky operations but continued to minimize American troop levels. Military success encouraged political progress, both at the Bonn Conference and as multiethnic Afghan forces occupied Kabul. Even with the initial lack of confidence at the principal level and the absence of contingency plans, Rumsfeld now claimed that the war proceeded "exactly as planned."[51] Indeed, November proved exemplary; within a month, a small number of CIA and SOF had utilized precision-guided munitions to help create an indigenous defeat of the Taliban. Few questioned this city-centric approach. Defeating the Taliban in the major cities of Afghanistan may have enabled American efforts to focus on al Qaeda, but many people treated this progress not as a means of winning the war but as victory itself. According to Michael Scheuer, "The military was really focused on taking cities, and that was kind of their definition of what victory would be."[52] Nonetheless, the events of November moved the United States closer to defeating and destroying al Qaeda.

7

DISTRACTIONS

November 27 to December 2, 2001

Could Iraq somehow have been involved?

— CONDOLEEZZA RICE[1]

The consideration of whether to use military force against Saddam Hussein's Iraq began to distract from the war in Afghanistan as early as November 21, 2001. The principals had briefly considered the possibility of Iraqi involvement immediately after the September 11 terrorist attacks. Interest in Iraq rapidly diminished when no evidence of a connection emerged. However, Iraq reentered the debate in late November when the model for regime change in Afghanistan appeared to succeed. Ultimately, the discourse over military action in Iraq diverted the attention of America's top military and civilian leaders at the most critical time of the war effort in Afghanistan.

The first mention of Iraq came one day after 9/11. At an NSC meeting on September 12, Rumsfeld raised the possibility of military action against Iraq. He argued that since Iraq remained a known sponsor of terrorism, any war on terrorism must confront the issue of Iraq. Powell reminded the group that al Qaeda—not Iraq—had just struck American soil. The next day, Shelton and Powell spoke and agreed that clear evidence linking Iraq to 9/11 remained the only legitimate premise for military action. According to Douglas Feith, "Iraq was on the minds of many Administration officials [at the September 14 NSC meeting]. . . . A global war on terrorism would, at some point, involve some kind of showdown with Iraq."[2] The most hawkish advocate for regime change in Iraq was Paul Wolfowitz. At Camp David on September 15, Wolfowitz exploited the fear of the Soviet experience in Afghanistan and argued that Saddam Hussein appeared easier to topple. Powell once again intervened, mentioning that aggression against Iraq would destroy any effort to maintain international support. Wolfowitz's interjection clearly irritated the president, who at the end of the meeting told his chief of staff, Andrew Card, to instruct Wolfowitz not to do so again.[3] Later that weekend, Cheney sided with Powell, Tenet, and Card by arguing that the current situation did not justify military action against Iraq. Although Rumsfeld appeared undecided, Wolfowitz remained the sole advocate for attacking Iraq. Condoleezza Rice recalled the discussion about Iraq:

> After September 11, the strategic calculation on Iraq changed, but only after we had a sound policy in Afghanistan and fully came to understand the transnational, post-9/11 threats the United States now faced. On September 12, we all asked ourselves, *could Iraq somehow have been involved?* We knew Saddam was implacable in his hatred of the United States. We knew he had tried to assassinate the President's father. So naturally, our thoughts turned to Iraq after the attacks, but not in a way that would change our national policy. Iraq did come up in the early War Council meetings, but it was generally in the same way Iraq came up in the first eight months of the Administration, that is in relation to smart sanctions. Iraq policy really did not change until . . . after the diplomatic efforts of 2002–2003 had failed. At this time, the President was most concerned with bringing Osama bin Laden to justice, defeating Al-Qaeda, and defending the homeland from future terrorist attacks.[4]

The debate over immediate action against Iraq had ended on September 17 when Bush said, "I believe Iraq was involved [in the September 11 attacks], but I'm not going to strike them now. I don't have the evidence at this point."[5]

But in the immediate aftermath of a successful, mostly indigenous, and swift regime change operation in Afghanistan, the perceived success of the "Afghan model" proved enticing. On November 21, just a week after Kabul fell, Rumsfeld told General Myers, "the President wants to know what kind of operations plan we have for Iraq."[6] Myers told Rumsfeld that OPLAN 1003, the war plan for Iraq, was out of date. The plan required around five hundred thousand troops to amass in theater over seven months before the war could begin. After the apparent success of the Afghan model in just over ten weeks and with only a few hundred troops, OPLAN 1003 seemed fundamentally flawed. Rumsfeld responded, "The President and I want to dust off that plan, bring it up to date. Let's schedule a call to General Franks for early next week."[7] That call to Franks took place on November 27 as he was planning the air campaign for Tora Bora. Myers was at CENTCOM headquarters with Franks when the call took place. Franks concurred with Myers about the state of OPLAN 1003. Rumsfeld told Franks, "Please dust it [OPLAN 1003] off and get back to me next week."[8] Exactly one week later, Franks briefed President Bush on the updated strategy for war in Iraq. Just as General Franks began to focus on attacking bin Laden's most likely location, the president's orders required him to focus his efforts on updating a two-hundred-page war plan (with a six-hundred-page appendix) according to a recently developed and practically untested model.[9]

8

A BATTLE WON
AND A WAR LOST

December 3 to December 22, 2001

There is only one result that counts: final victory. Until then,
nothing is decided, nothing won, and nothing lost.

— CARL VON CLAUSEWITZ, ON WAR[1]

By December 3, Operation Enduring Freedom had nearly achieved its objectives. With the Taliban in retreat across Afghanistan, efforts at the operational level shifted toward pursuing al Qaeda. This shift aligned with the military's push to capture the southern Taliban strongholds, while the CIA committed resources exclusively to tracking bin Laden. But besides displacing al Qaeda, the war had done little to threaten the fundamental existence of the terrorist organization. The key to victory—yet to be attained—was destroying al Qaeda's leadership. The best opportunity to eliminate al Qaeda's nucleus occurred at the Battle of Tora Bora during the first half of December. This battle gained notoriety for the tactical and operational errors that led to bin Laden's escape. Critics argue that these failures stemmed from America's reliance on dubious Afghan warlords, Pakistan's lackluster effort to seal the border, military risk aversion, the diversion of senior military leaders to revamp the Iraq war plans, and Gen. Tommy Franks's operational decision not to deploy more American troops to the battle or seal off the escape routes.[2] But beyond these legitimate criticisms lies a startling truth: the failures at Tora Bora were as much the result of policy miscalculations by America's top civilian leaders as tactical errors made by Franks and his subordinate military commanders.

Gary Berntsen dispatched two intelligence officers, a special operations soldier, and an Air Force combat controller into the mountains of Tora Bora to establish a preliminary observation point in the first days of December. The men were part of the team deployed by Berntsen to Jalalabad the week before. But as intelligence traced bin Laden's movements southward from Jalalabad to Tora Bora, Berntsen ordered the team to follow. Hazrat Ali, a local warlord in eastern Afghanistan, would assist the team in traveling from Jalalabad to Tora Bora. Upon arrival of the local escorts, the four Americans were surprised to discover that Ali had sent three of his sixteen-year-old cousins to guide the first U.S. team into al Qaeda's greatest stronghold. Nonetheless, the team proceeded.[3]

Even without knowing the age of the Afghan liaisons, Col. John Mulholland, the commander of the Fifth Special Forces Group in Afghanistan, considered the mission in eastern Afghanistan to be so risky that he refused to attach an ODA. Despite knowing that bin Laden was the primary objective, Mulholland told Berntsen, "Send your team in. If in a week they're still alive and operating, I'll send a team to work with them."[4] Team Juliet immediately assembled a few local warlords into an impromptu Eastern Alliance to pursue bin Laden. After a brief delay when rocket-propelled grenades improperly packed on a mule detonated and killed two Afghan guides, the four men of Team Juliet advanced into the mountains as the first Americans dedicated to hunting bin Laden after 9/11.[5]

The ragtag Eastern Alliance consisted of several Pashtun warlords with no previous relationship to the CIA. Hazrat Ali and Hajji Mohammed Zaman Ghamsharik led the two predominant but rival tribes that American forces depended on both at Tora Bora and in Jalalabad. While the Northern Alliance had suggested Ali as a potential ally to Gary Berntsen, Pakistan endorsed Zaman. A former mujahideen commander during the Soviet invasion, Zaman had returned from a self-imposed exile in Dijon, France, to rally resistance against the Taliban just after the September 11 terrorist attacks. A third contingent of forces was commanded by Hajji Zahir Qadir, another rival of Zaman. Qadir had spent years in jail during the Taliban era until he escaped with Herati warlord Ismail Khan in 1999. From 1992 to 1996, Qadir's father, Abdul Qadir, was the governor of Nangarhar, the eastern province of Afghanistan that includes Jalalabad and Tora Bora. Abdul Qadir was also the brother of Abdul Haq, the Pashtun warlord who was tortured and killed by the Taliban when trying to enter Afghanistan on October 26, 2001. Abdul Qadir would become one of Afghanistan's vice presidents shortly after Hamid Karzai took office, only to be assassinated a few months later. Although the identity of Abdul Qadir's assassin remains uncertain, Zaman is suspected of orchestrating the attack and dispatching his cousin to assassinate the vice president.[6]

The military, which typically relied on the CIA for information about local factions, asked Berntsen about the reliability of these tribal leaders. To Berntsen "it was clear that the men leading this new Afghan force did not have the same desire we did to pursue and destroy al-Qaeda."[7] (In his book Berntsen refers to Ali and Zaman as "Babrak" and "Nuruddin," respectively.) But despite the concerns that they harbored, both the CIA and the U.S. military chose to rely upon the Eastern Alliance. Berntsen later explained the predicament:

> We were in search of allies. . . . They [the Northern Alliance] put me in contact with Babrak [Ali]. So that was the bridge to the other guys. And then Nuruddin [Zaman] shows up, but he had already made contact with the U.S. in Pakistan, and then he appears, just as we are doing this stuff. So we thought, okay—he has fighters too. . . . I had to go down [to Jalalabad and Tora Bora] alone. I had to assemble these guys. I had to pay these guys. . . . I'm not sure how much help I am going to get [from the military] at that point. I'm optimistic, but I'm not sure. So I took all comers.[8]

Team Juliet's plan of attack at Tora Bora depended entirely on Eastern Alliance forces for its success. The operation intended to trap bin Laden and his fighters by forcing them against the fifteen-thousand-foot peaks separating Pakistan from Afghanistan. Eastern Alliance forces would deploy along the eastern and western flanks while American forces would approach from the north and direct airpower to push the enemy southward. With the flanks properly sealed to hinder escape through the valleys meandering into Pakistan, al Qaeda could either traverse the grueling mountains or stay and fight. But the CIA officers in Tora Bora and Kabul realized that the only way to prevent eventual escape required securing the southern border with a number of reliable and well-trained troops. On the evening of December 3, Berntsen issued a formal request for eight hundred Army Rangers to block the escape routes and assist in the Battle of Tora Bora.[9] Hank Crumpton passed Berntsen's request to the CIA leadership and General Franks. Circling back, Crumpton soon told Berntsen, "I doubt it will happen. General Franks wants to stick with what has worked, our small teams with our Afghan allies. He also says it would take time to plan. Time to deploy rangers. Too much time."[10]

Berntsen's aggressive style both benefited and detracted from the war effort. By getting an interagency team into Jalalabad and Tora Bora, his willingness to take risks offered tremendous rewards. But Berntsen tended to act first and request permission later. He deployed the CIA team to Jalalabad without the requisite approval from CIA headquarters. Likewise, when the four men of Team Juliet reached an observation point over the active al Qaeda camp in the Milawa Valley of Tora Bora, Berntsen immediately granted them permission to begin the aerial assault. Starting December 4, the team continuously directed nearly seven hundred thousand pounds of ordnance onto the Milawa stronghold for more than fifty-six hours, causing the remaining al Qaeda fighters to abandon it and withdraw deeper into the mountains. A day after the bombardments began, Crumpton called Berntsen from CTC headquarters and said, "It's apparent that you have a team up near Tora Bora and they're calling in a lot of air strikes. . . . Good for you. Based on the intel and intercepts from our end it appears that bin Laden is up there, too."[11]

Although the battle killed many Taliban and al Qaeda operatives and forced a tactical retreat from Milawa, patiently developing a more coordinated effort with reliable partners might have provided a better outcome. The spontaneous beginning of the Battle of Tora Bora cost American forces the element of surprise and left them without sufficient troops to adequately pursue and contain al Qaeda as it retreated deeper into the mountains and closer to Pakistan.

Berntsen later explained the rationale behind the aggressive approach to the battle at Milawa:

> You make those decisions to do that . . . it's all based on intel [intelligence]. It's an intel-driven conflict. It's not improvisation. It's execution based on intel immediately. And fast. And it's all about speed. . . . Our ability to adjust; their ability not to know what's happening. . . .

No one was able to think that fast [in determining the best approach to the battle at Milawa]. My point was that in each engagement, I'm trying to bring force to bear to eliminate al Qaeda's leadership. They're in those elements, and I'm attacking them. Yeah, the possibility exists that they be pushed back to the border and eventually slip through, but I've got to take the shot while I've got it. . . .

My view on that was I had to take a shot each time because I may kill him [bin Laden] on this one. I may kill him today, or I may kill him tomorrow, when I've got him there.[12]

The actions of the four men from Team Juliet generated enough pressure for Colonel Mulholland to dispatch ODA 572 to Tora Bora on December 6. But the SF team deployed under specific rules not to directly engage the enemy but only to observe and direct air support in "terminal guidance operations." On December 2, Maj. Gen. Dell Dailey from Task Force Sword deployed forty special operations commandos to link up with Hazrat Ali of the Eastern Alliance in Jalalabad and move to Tora Bora to facilitate killing bin Laden.[13] The team of forty SOF commandos was sent instead of the eight hundred Rangers that Berntsen had requested.[14]

Meanwhile, as Franks briefed Bush on the updated war plan for Iraq, delegates of the Bonn Conference selected Hamid Karzai as the prime minister of the Afghan Interim Authority. On December 5, five minutes before receiving notification of his nomination, Karzai narrowly evaded death when a two-thousand-pound bomb from an American warplane accidentally dropped on his location near Kandahar, killing three SOF soldiers. The battle for Kandahar also progressed rapidly. After weeks of bombardments and fighting, Sherzai and ODA 583 captured Kandahar on December 7, liberating the last major Taliban stronghold.[15]

On the same day that Kandahar fell, American forces and intelligence officers regrouped at the northern outskirts of Tora Bora. Meanwhile, Hajji Zaman Ghamsharik attempted to negotiate a surrender by al Qaeda and initiated a ceasefire in direct contradiction to CIA and SOF directives. Berntsen furiously called CENTCOM to redirect airpower on al Qaeda positions and undermine the ceasefire. Fearing that the Eastern Alliance would change sides and allow al Qaeda to escape, Berntsen repeated his heretofore ignored request for eight hundred Rangers to individuals at CIA and CENTCOM headquarters. The members of the Eastern Alliance appeared increasingly unreliable and ineffective. Worse, with the start of Ramadan, the Afghans returned to their homes at night to break the fast, ceding any territorial gains from the day's fighting.[16]

On December 8, command for the Battle of Tora Bora shifted from the CIA to Dalton Fury, the author of *Kill Bin Laden: A Delta Force Commander's Account of the Hunt for the World's Most Wanted Man* and the leader of the forty-man special operations contingent sent as a substitute for the eight hundred Rangers that Berntsen had requested. Over the next two days, Fury and his team surveyed the front lines and established observation posts, patiently developing a coordinated assault. They discovered that al Qaeda maintained the tactical advantage with superb observation points, hidden mortar positions, and multiple defensive posts. Given ODA 572's limited ability to engage the enemy, Fury ordered them to establish two observation posts on the eastern and western ridgelines. Hazrat Ali told Fury that several caves held Soviet tanks. Two special operations snipers later confirmed this nearly impossible scenario, reporting that al Qaeda had somehow managed to drive the tanks up the steep, jagged mountains and position them deep inside large caves. By December 9, Fury and his team of forty special operations personnel and fourteen Special Forces soldiers, six intelligence officers, and a few Air Force combat controllers initiated the next phase of the Battle of Tora Bora.[17]

A fifteen-thousand-pound BLU-82 Daisy Cutter commenced the renewed effort on the morning of December 9. One of the Eastern Alliance troops who delivered food to al Qaeda during the brief ceasefire provided the location and description of a group of men who appeared to include Osama bin Laden and Ayman al Zawahiri. Berntsen considered this the perfect opportunity to exhibit American airpower to the Eastern Alliance, but the BLU-82 disappointed. Not only did it fail to detonate fully, it landed nearly a thousand meters from its intended target. Later that day, Fury sent Team Kilo to assume command of ODA 572's observation posts and reposition them closer to the enemy's current location. The rest of the team would act as a quick reaction force in case bin Laden was spotted. Two special operations snipers from Kilo team directed bombs onto al Qaeda positions for thirteen hours upon arriving at one of the two observation points.[18]

December 10 was one of the most eventful days in Tora Bora. It began as the four other members of Team Kilo departed for ODA 572's second observation

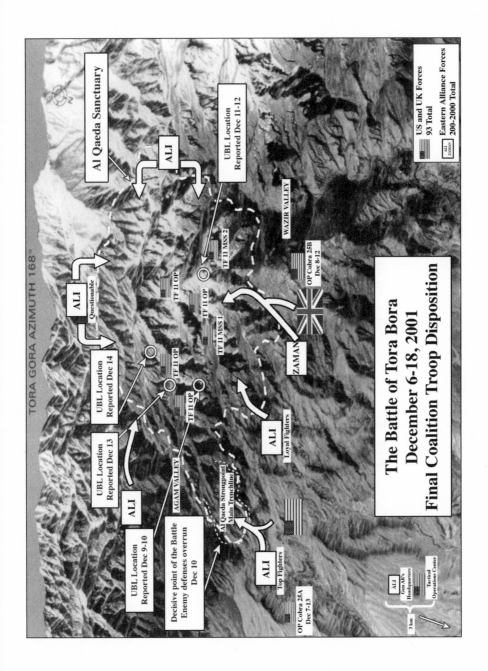

TORA GORA AZIMUTH 168°

Al Qaeda Sanctuary

ALI

ALI

ALI
Questionable

UBL Location
Reported Dec 14

UBL Location
Reported Dec 13

UBL Location
Reported Dec 9-10

ALI

Decisive point of the Battle
Enemy defenses overrun
Dec 10

AGAM VALLEY

Al Qaeda Strongpoint
Main Trenchline

ALI
Top Fighters

OP Cobra 25A
Dec 7-13

UBL Location
Reported Dec 11-12

TF 11 OP

TF 11 OP

TF 11 MSS 2

TF 11 OP

TF 11 MSS 1

TF 11 OP

WAZIR VALLEY

OP Cobra 25B
Dec 8-12

ZAMAN

ALI
Loyal Fighters

The Battle of Tora Bora
December 6-18, 2001
Final Coalition Troop Disposition

US and UK Forces
93 Total

Eastern Alliance Forces
200-2000 Total
ALI
ZAMAN

ALI
Gen Ali's
Headquarters

Tactical
Operations Center

3 km

93

point. Contrary to his previous timidity, Hazrat Ali relayed to Fury that he would attack a recently discovered al Qaeda vulnerability. One special operations soldier, an Air Force combat controller, and CIA officer Adam Khan accompanied Ali and his men. As the four men from Team Kilo arrived at the observation point, Ali and the American contingent pushed through heavy small-arms and mortar fire. The three Americans, backed by close air support and a dwindling number of Afghan troops, penetrated farther into Tora Bora than any other American soldier thus far. Although mortar fire hindered their advance, Khan and the two commandos directed numerous devastating strikes on al Qaeda positions. Fury received notice of a signals intercept of an enemy transmission stating, "Father [bin Laden] is trying to break through the siege line."[19] The three Americans, now supported by only five Afghan allies, may have succeeded in flushing bin Laden from his hideout.[20]

And then it happened. Bin Laden made an egregious error. Under intense pressure from the bombing, he spent a few seconds too long on his radio. American intelligence intercepted the transmission and determined his location within ten meters. The chief CIA officer at Tora Bora passed the eight-digit grid location to Fury, who immediately mobilized the other thirty-two special operations commandos to hunt bin Laden. In compliance with orders, the commandos would meet Hazrat Ali and move forward together. But on their way to the battle, Ali's convoy passed them going the opposite direction. Instead of cordoning off bin Laden's location, Ali and his men were returning to their homes for the night. Fury also received notice that Khan and the two TF Sword soldiers had initiated escape-and-evasion maneuvers when an enemy machine gun flanked their position. The special operations cadre was twenty-five hundred meters from bin Laden's last known location when their Afghan drivers stopped, refusing to move closer to al Qaeda. Although Fury and his team were safe in their current position, small-arms fire trapped them between two ridges. With three men deep in enemy territory and no helpful Afghan guides to pursue bin Laden, Fury faced a tough decision. Special Operations Command had issued strict orders not to lead any assault on al Qaeda but only facilitate and exploit the Eastern Alliance's progress. After a few seconds, he told his commanders, "Okay, we'll have another shot at bin Laden. . . . We need to concentrate on recovering our boys first."[21] For the next nine years, no better opportunity to kill or capture bin Laden presented itself.

Without any new intelligence or Afghan guides, Fury decided to return for the night upon hearing that the three Americans were safe. CIA operative Khan and the two commandos had escaped just as the special operations forces began searching for them. In response to the pitiful effort of the Eastern Alliance the night before, Fury adjusted the operational functions of his forces to reflect the necessity for independent movement. He dispatched two larger groups of snipers, assaulters, and Air Force combat controllers to the eastern and western observation points as mission support site (MSS) teams. Also on December 11, eight British commandos from the Special Boat Service (SBS) arrived to support the American troops. Khan informed Fury that bin Laden had flooded the local villages with cash, and the bribes had reached some members of the Eastern Alliance. Ever the rivals, Zaman's and Ali's forces competed in the afternoon to control a hill overlooking al Qaeda's position. To Ali's dismay, Zaman and his forces arrived first at the apex. A twenty-five-man team of special operations forces and British SBS commandos attempted to covertly infiltrate to the hilltop to direct close air support but were forced to turn around to prevent the discovery of the Western troops by journalists in the area. Despite the substantial tonnage dropped that day, no American ground troops managed to advance from their current location. The MSS team redeployed around midnight to avoid the press. They arrived at the newly controlled hilltop to support Zaman's eighty troops during the early morning hours, but the MSS team entered a far different situation from what they expected.[22]

Unbeknownst to any American, Zaman had again opened negotiations with al Qaeda just after capturing the hilltop on December 11. By the time that the MSS team arrived on December 12, he had initiated a ceasefire while al Qaeda had purportedly agreed to surrender. To the Americans, the surrender appeared to be a diversion. But when the twenty-five soldiers began to establish offensive positions to direct air support, Zaman's eighty troops raised their weapons and forced the Americans to withdraw from the crest. News of the surrender enraged Berntsen, who vehemently tried to undermine the ceasefire. Above the snow-capped peaks of the Hindu Kush, an American fighter pilot engaged his afterburners and drew "ON 8" in the sky, referring to the surrender deadline for the following morning. Dressed up in a brown suit and silver hat, Zaman visited Fury and pompously declared, "This is the greatest day in the history of Afghanistan. . . . Bin Laden is finished."[23] Infuriated by Zaman's naïveté, the

Americans broke the ceasefire at five in the afternoon, this time without encountering resistance from Zaman's fighters. The MSS team moved forward into the mountains of Tora Bora and began to engage the enemy. The commandos turned on their night-vision goggles as darkness fell over the sierra and directed a loitering AC-130 gunship to destroy enemy targets. Armed with a side-facing 20mm Gatling gun and a 40mm cannon to complement the forearm-length shells of its 105mm M102 howitzer, AC-130 gunships had become devastating weapons after the military shifted to close air support in early November. By 8:00 the next morning, no al Qaeda fighter had surrendered, but quite a few lay dead as a result of the MSS team assault. Nonetheless, American intelligence estimated that up to eight hundred al Qaeda fighters used the diversion to escape into Pakistan.[24]

The night of December 13, 2001—the Muslim holiday Leilat al-Qadr—marked the fourteenth anniversary of bin Laden's victory at Jaji.[25] American forces continued to advance into Tora Bora. The second MSS team infiltrated into enemy territory while U.S. warplanes relentlessly attacked al Qaeda positions. Four more British SBS commandos also joined the fight. Meanwhile, signals intercepts exposed intensifying chaos within al Qaeda's ranks. Speaking in formal Arabic prose, bin Laden told his followers, "Our prayers have not been answered. Times are dire. . . . I'm sorry for getting you involved in this battle, if you can no longer resist, you may surrender with my blessing."[26] But Hajji Zaman Ghamsharik's unfulfilled surrender agreement increasingly appeared to be a distraction orchestrated to let the enemy escape. With over fifty American and British commandos pushing forward tenaciously, al Qaeda continued to retreat south toward Pakistan.[27]

Just as al Qaeda and Taliban operatives began to flee from Tora Bora, an international incident arose that detracted from the already modest Pakistani effort to seal the border. In accordance with the diplomatic push after 9/11, Pakistan had deployed four thousand troops to secure parts of the Afghan border. But on December 13, five armed Pakistani nationals assaulted the Indian parliament building with the intent to kill as many parliamentarians as possible. The attack failed, and Indian security forces quickly killed the militants. Intelligence soon identified the assailants as members of Jaish-e-Mohammed (JeM), a regional terrorist organization with long-standing ties to both Pakistan's ISI and al Qaeda. Bruce Riedel observed the events unfold from his position on the National Security Council:

India was quick to find connections between the five and Pakistan's infamous Inter-Services Intelligence Directorate, the ISI. The five attackers were Pakistani citizens and members of the ISI-supported, if not created, Jaish-e-Mohammad (JeM) terror organisation. The JeM was founded by Maulana Masood Azhar, a long-time terrorist who was freed in December 1999 from an Indian jail in return for the release of the hostages from the hijacked Indian Airlines flight 814 taken to Kandahar by Kashmiri terrorists backed by the ISI. The ISI took Azhar on a victory tour through Pakistan to raise money to create the JeM.[28]

Relations between India and Pakistan deteriorated rapidly and bilateral mobilizations for war ensued. Pakistan immediately repositioned most of its troops on the Afghanistan-Pakistan border to its border with India. U.S. attention at the upper levels of government quickly shifted from the war in Afghanistan to defusing the precarious situation. Between the largest mobilization in India's history and Pakistan's refusal to sever relations with JeM and other regional terrorist organizations, the two nuclear-armed neighbors would sit at the brink of war for the following year.[29] Nonetheless, the terrorist incident removed the sole military force sealing the border and undermined the tactical progress Western commandos were making in the Battle of Tora Bora.

The end was near on December 14, but its terms remained undetermined. Over the last three days, American and British commandos had advanced several thousand meters into enemy territory. Eastern Alliance troops moved along the eastern and western flanks of the battle to trap al Qaeda. Expecting to die imminently, bin Laden wrote his will. At noon some of Hazrat Ali's fighters observed a tall individual enter a cave with fifty escorts. American intelligence intercepted what would become bin Laden's last radio transmission. But the bureaucratic leadership in Washington and Afghanistan did not comprehend the fragility of the situation. As bin Laden began his escape, the CIA replaced Berntsen as the chief Agency officer for northern and eastern Afghanistan. Colonel Mulholland, the commander of the Fifth Special Forces Group, placed such strict limitations on the ODA team at Tora Bora—in accordance with his orders—that he essentially removed them from the battle. While Pakistan relocated troops from the Afghan border to its border with India, CENTCOM continued to ignore Berntsen's request for more troops to seal the southern edge.[30]

The commandos met occasional pockets of al Qaeda resistance as they continued their assault on December 15. In the afternoon, Eastern Alliance troops observed someone similar in appearance to bin Laden traveling with dozens of al Qaeda fighters. The closest Air Force combat controller directed all available aircraft to attack the position. Meanwhile, three Army special operations snipers climbed up a steep cliff into an ideal observation point and continuously directed close air support from the precipice for two days. At night, the three snipers discovered that their position corresponded to an al Qaeda escape route, so they hid on the vertical bluff as dozens of enemy fighters passed by overhead. In the late afternoon on the last day of Ramadan, bin Laden divided his troops in half for the final escape.[31] A group of 135 men would head eastward through a longer path into Pakistan while bin Laden and 200 Saudi and Yemeni fighters crossed the high, unforgiving peaks of the Hindu Kush in a direct route to Parachinar, a provincial capital in Pakistan's Federally Administered Tribal Areas inside Parrot's Beak.[32]

The Battle of Tora Bora drew to a close on the afternoon of December 16. While a few al Qaeda operatives continued to fight, most had already fled Tora Bora and disappeared into the tribal regions of Pakistan. A few combatants surrendered. Over the fourteen-day battle, ninety-three Western commandos had directed over 1,650 bombs onto al Qaeda positions. But special operations commander Dalton Fury likened the battle to "working in an invisible cage."[33] Despite the presence of the best-trained assault troops in the American military, the only weapon used to kill the enemy was airpower. Just as bin Laden trekked across the treacherous mountain passes toward Pakistan, Secretary of Defense Donald Rumsfeld arrived at Bagram Air Base on the morning of December 16. Soon after Rumsfeld's arrival, Fury received instructions from Maj. Gen. Dell Dailey at Bagram to query Hazrat Ali about a buildup of conventional troops in Tora Bora, presumably to contain and destroy al Qaeda elements still in the mountains.[34] But it was too late.

Osama bin Laden had escaped.

Although the exact details of his flight remain a mystery, bin Laden left the mountains of Tora Bora sometime between December 14 and December 16 and traversed directly over the highest peaks to enter Pakistan. Without adequate forces to seal the southern border, escape was almost inevitable. Once in Pakistan, bin Laden most likely traveled to Parachinar. From there, he disappeared.

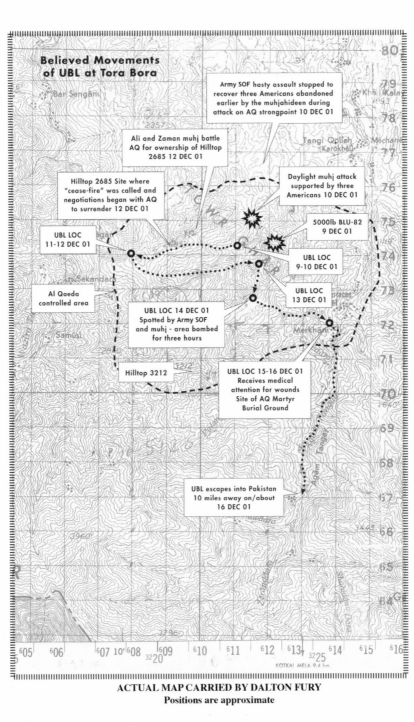

Believed Movements of UBL at Tora Bora

Army SOF hasty assault stopped to recover three Americans abandoned earlier by the muhjahideen during attack on AQ strongpoint 10 DEC 01

Ali and Zaman muhj battle AQ for ownership of Hilltop 2685 12 DEC 01

Hilltop 2685 Site where "cease-fire" was called and negotiations began with AQ to surrender 12 DEC 01

Daylight muhj attack supported by three Americans 10 DEC 01

5000lb BLU-82 9 DEC 01

UBL LOC 11-12 DEC 01

UBL LOC 9-10 DEC 01

UBL LOC 13 DEC 01

Al Qaeda controlled area

UBL LOC 14 DEC 01 Spotted by Army SOF and muhj - area bombed for three hours

Hilltop 3212

UBL LOC 15-16 DEC 01 Receives medical attention for wounds Site of AQ Martyr Burial Ground

UBL escapes into Pakistan 10 miles away on/about 16 DEC 01

ACTUAL MAP CARRIED BY DALTON FURY
Positions are approximate

President Bush recalled in his memoirs, "If we had ever known where he [Osama bin Laden] was, we would have moved heaven and earth to bring him to justice."[35] Yet during those frigid days in mid-December in the unforgiving mountains of Tora Bora, it seemed that heaven and earth parted to allow bin Laden to escape.

The symbolism of bin Laden's legendary escape from the world's most powerful military on the last nights of Ramadan radiated across the Islamic world. That critical moments in both the Battle of Jaji and the Battle of Tora Bora occurred at the end of Ramadan must have signified divine intervention to bin Laden and his followers. Michael Scheuer has pointed out that "in terms of an Islamic world that knows its history, the fact that he escaped in August of 1998 from the cruise missile attack, [and] that we didn't get him at Tora Bora [suggests] . . . that there is something about this man . . . that is blessed by God."[36]

The Battle of Tora Bora was first and foremost a tactical failure. The failure to prevent the exodus of hundreds—if not thousands—of core al Qaeda and Taliban leaders and operatives into Pakistan represented a catastrophic blunder that enabled America's enemies to regroup and endure in relative safety. This operational failure stemmed largely from the light-footprint approach used to topple the Taliban across Afghanistan. The low number of American commandos, backed by the full force of U.S. air power, and combined with dubious Afghan allies was an effective formula for disrupting and removing the political power of local Taliban forces in Afghanistan. But this model of warfare was neither designed nor suitable for cordoning off swaths of land and capturing or killing the enemies within that region.

It was a classic ends-and-means mismatch. The small SOF-centric footprint would effectively push al Qaeda and the Taliban out of Tora Bora as it was designed to do, but forcing America's enemies into Pakistan occurred instead and at the expense of destroying its core leadership. The orders received by the military commanders in the battle reflected the disconnect between tactics and strategy. Dalton Fury's top priorities at Tora Bora were "(1) kill/capture UBL [Osama bin Laden], (2) align with and secure guides from the Eastern Alliance Opposition Group, and (3) penetrate AQ's [al Qaeda's] defenses."[37] But despite these priorities, "our higher headquarters had repeatedly directed us *not* to spearhead any assault on bin Laden's cave sanctuary. Our job was to facilitate the muhj [mujahideen – Eastern Alliance] advance, follow closely behind, and be in a position to exploit their progress."[38] Colonel Mulholland, who commanded all Special Forces ODAs in Afghanistan, including ODA 572 at Tora Bora, viewed the operation as a "flawed concept,"[39] stating in an interview:

I was concerned about the inadequacy of the force to the mission at hand. . . . I did give that team specific guidance to support the Afghan forces, provide classic advisory assistance to them, and to provide close air support. . . . If our team had specific insight where bin Laden was, I'd have been happy for our team to go after him and get him, but recognizing that they were part of a larger effort, with specific elements from our military and government that were specifically charged with the mission of finding bin Laden. So that wasn't our specific mission, nor was I asked to have teams specifically charged with that mission. That's not what I was asked to provide.[40]

Between the limitations placed on Fury's special operations contingent by Major General Dailey, the commander of Task Force Sword, and those placed on Colonel Mulholland's ODA 572 by CENTCOM commander General Franks, no part of the U.S. government—including the troops at Tora Bora—was tasked with sealing the mountainous region and subsequently killing or capturing the enemy at Tora Bora.[41]

Even with the light-footprint approach, Franks never reinforced the ninety-three commandos at Tora Bora. In an in-depth study on the feasibility of conducting a block-and-sweep operation at Tora Bora, Peter Krause, a PhD candidate in the Security Studies Program at the Massachusetts Institute of Technology, concluded:

The insertion of highly trained, well-equipped U.S. forces as both hammer and anvil in its block and sweep . . . combined with the superior airpower . . . would have significantly increased the likelihood of more enemy killed, fewer total casualties (although perhaps more American casualties due simply to a greater percentage of American troops), and more territory taken in less time.[42]

Berntsen never received a response to his request for eight hundred Rangers, although his message may have reached the highest levels of government. In a conversation between Crumpton and Franks over Berntsen's request, Crumpton warned that the situation at Tora Bora was different from defeating the Taliban, but Franks argued that the success of the small footprint and the mobilization time for additional troops outweighed a change in the current approach.[43] "When this [request for eight hundred Rangers] was denied, they sent us instead," Fury recalled.[44] The low number of U.S. troops, their risk-averse orders as dictated by their commanders, the reliance on questionable Afghan allies, and the lack of U.S. troops to reinforce the battle or seal the southern border between Tora Bora and Pakistan allowed a large contingent of the enemy to escape unscathed.

An effective tactic to augment the light-footprint approach taken at Tora Bora would have been to seal the border between Tora Bora and Pakistan's tribal areas with U.S. troops. When President Bush asked Crumpton in the Oval Office in late November or early December whether the Pakistani effort to secure the borders had been adequate, he replied, "No sir. No one has enough troops to prevent any possibility of escape in a region like that."[45] Indeed, Crumpton had brought a topographical map that CIA cartographers had specially devised to indicate the escape routes from Afghanistan into Pakistan. The map indicated that "the enemy could slip into Pakistan almost anywhere."[46] Crumpton told the president, "With such a long border, rough terrain, high elevation, no army on earth can seal this. We could deploy recon units, combined with imagery assets, to monitor the most likely routes of enemy retreat. But with such a vast territory and uncertain weather, we could miss their escape."[47]

But while Crumpton's answer was accurate, it was not applicable to Tora Bora. Although it would require an inordinate number of troops to seal the fifteen-hundred-mile Afghanistan-Pakistan border, it would have taken only a few hundred to a couple thousand troops to secure the six-mile stretch of Tora Bora. At the time, one thousand troops from the Tenth Mountain Division were stationed at K2 in Uzbekistan; Brig. Gen. James Mattis commanded twelve hundred Marines from Fifteenth and the Twenty-sixth Marine Expeditionary Units at Camp Rhino near Kandahar; and Special Forces, SEAL, and Army special operations teams continued to operate across the country.

Mattis asked to reposition his forces to seal the border at Tora Bora. With his force of twelve hundred, Mattis could have positioned one Marine every eight meters across the entire southern border of Tora Bora.[48] Speaking later entirely in speculative terms, General Mattis stated, "Hypothetically, there is a way [to block bin Laden's escape]. If you had good intel about where he was—the approximate area—there are only so many ways out."[49]

Furthermore, Dalton Fury considered the ideal approach to the Battle of Tora Bora to include an assault from the south:

> Coming from the south had great potential, was UBL's [Osama bin Laden's] back door where he committed zero pax [personnel] to the defense, and would have allowed us to already be higher than the AQ [al Qaeda] positions. Had the muhj [mujahideen – Eastern Alliance] pushed from the north as they did, with us in the south on higher ground, UBL and AQ would have been pinned in with very little room to maneuver in that steep terrain. Without this option, using any force, Rangers, Marines, Tenth Mountain, in the south to cut off their escape paths would have been plausible as their presence would have been unknown to the muhj fighters [we] were linked with.[50]

Nonetheless, Fury continues, "COO [Concept of the Operation] was definitely shaped by the guidance [from above] as it prevented us from approaching AQ positions from the south, the PK [Pakistan] side of Tora Bora."[51] Berntsen thought Fury's plan to approach from the south was a good idea and was willing to insert Fury's troops using a CIA-operated Mi-17 helicopter. However, according to Berntsen, Fury was "turned down by his own people."[52] The logistics for these operations would have been challenging but by no means prohibitive.[53] Although it is impossible to predict what would have happened had the Bush administration adopted any of these approaches, these tactical maneuvers would have made it substantially harder for al Qaeda and Taliban forces to escape from Tora Bora.

And while no faction in the Eastern Alliance acted as an adequate substitute for U.S. forces, one of the three major warlords proved to be more than unreliable. Hajji Zaman Ghamsharik twice enabled al Qaeda operatives to escape Tora Bora by implementing unilateral ceasefires and obstructing

American assaults, the latter instance at gunpoint. Berntsen would subsequently conclude that contacting Zaman was "the biggest mistake I made in the deployment."[54] As the fog of war dissipated over the mountains of Tora Bora, Zaman became a primary suspect in aiding bin Laden's escape. Both Hazrat Ali and Hajji Zahir Qadir repeatedly and sternly warned the CIA that Hajji Zaman Ghamsharik was a treacherous ally. "Babrak [Hazrat Ali] and Hajji Zahir with limited resources did the best they could," Berntsen recalled. "Nuruddin [Hajji Zaman Ghamsharik] was the guy who we believe cooperated with the Pakistanis and is the guy that allowed bin Laden to get out."[55]

Ultimately, General Franks remained committed to the light-footprint approach and refused to deploy additional troops to Tora Bora. Franks denied both Berntsen's and Mattis's requests to insert supplementary American forces into the Battle of Tora Bora. Franks expressed concern that dedicating additional American troops would take weeks to deploy and result in lost momentum or even bin Laden's escape. But thousands of troops remained in theater and able to deploy on a moment's notice, and Fury's team, backed by close air support and the Eastern Alliance, represented the only force pushing bin Laden into Pakistan. Lt. Gen. Michael DeLong, Franks's deputy at CENTCOM, expressed another concern that reflected Franks's axiom of studying the Soviet strategy and doing the opposite. DeLong argued that the population near Tora Bora remained sympathetic to bin Laden, and any attempt to infiltrate conventional troops to the region would instill anger and result in firefights with the Afghan locals. Fury contends that, "Had just one of the thousands of bombs dropped in those two weeks killed UBL [Osama bin Laden], nobody would be Monday-morning-quarterbacking the decision to use a small SOF-centric footprint. Instead, everyone would be calling President Bush and Rumsfeld heroes."[56] Nonetheless, the United States should never have relegated matters of such vital strategic importance to mere chance alone. And despite the overwhelming evidence and direct experiences of CIA and military officers on the battlefield, in 2004 Franks wrongly asserted, "We don't know to this day whether Mr. bin Laden was at Tora Bora in December 2001."[57]

The Battle of Tora Bora was also a failure of policy. General Franks's attitude and decisions were a direct reflection of the guidance he received from the civilian leadership. President George W. Bush considered the goal of Operation

Enduring Freedom to be "removing al Qaeda's safe haven in Afghanistan."[58] This broad objective propagated down the chain of command assumedly through General Franks to Col. John Mulholland, who viewed his mission as the commander of the Fifth Special Forces Group to be to "remove Afghanistan as a sanctuary for al Qaeda."[59] The failure to clearly discriminate between removing Afghanistan as a haven for al Qaeda and destroying the terrorist organization and its leadership likely resulted in the reapplication of the light-footprint approach so as to achieve the former at the expense of the latter. The Battle of Tora Bora successfully removed al Qaeda from Afghanistan as ordered by President Bush, but the flight of bin Laden and his coterie into Pakistan reflected the inadequacy of this objective.

Beyond President Bush, the top three civilians at the Department of Defense discouraged a narrow focus on Osama bin Laden and al Qaeda in Afghanistan. Years later in his memoir, Defense Secretary Rumsfeld recalled, "The justification for our military operations in Afghanistan was not the capture or killing of one person. Our country's primary purpose was to try to prevent terrorists from attacking us again. There was far more to the threat posed by Islamist extremism than one man."[60] Under Secretary of Defense Feith explained the policy implications in more detail:

> We took bin Laden seriously, but we believed that the purposes of U.S. military action after 9/11 went beyond striking at the perpetrators. We felt compelled to choose a more ambitious strategic goal—to prevent further attacks that would kill Americans and compromise our security. And our immediate objectives were to disrupt terrorist operations and generate pressure on terrorism's state supporters. We had little faith—and not enough high-quality evidence—that even successful attacks on the few targets we could identify in Afghanistan would seriously obstruct terrorist operations in the near term.[61]

While Deputy Secretary Wolfowitz "warned against focusing narrowly on al Qaeda and Afghanistan," Rumsfeld instructed his civilian and military subordinates, "Don't over-elevate the importance of al Qaida."[62] From the perspective of these top officials, Osama bin Laden and his terrorist network in Afghanistan were not the fundamental target but merely actors in a much broader global conflict aimed to prevent terrorist attacks by whomever and wherever they arose.

President Bush's priorities for Operation Enduring Freedom also played a critical role in the outcome at Tora Bora. The NSC meeting on November 13—the day after Kabul fell—epitomized the president's priorities. At the meeting, Bush expressed how WMD targets took precedence over securing the Afghan border with Pakistan. His approach to killing bin Laden was, in his words, "If he moves elsewhere, we're just going to get him there."[63] At the time of the Battle of Tora Bora, one of the missions of the twelve hundred Marines commanded by Brigadier General Mattis was to support chemical, biological, radiological, and nuclear inspection teams around Kandahar.[64] So when Mattis approached his superior and asked to redirect his Marines to Tora Bora, the decision to deny his request reflected the priorities that President Bush had established in the November 13 NSC meeting and throughout the war. The failure to capture or kill Osama bin Laden at Tora Bora may have been an on-the-ground consequence of this statement of priorities.

The largest mistake made by President Bush and Secretary of Defense Rumsfeld during the first months of Operation Enduring Freedom—and more specifically the Battle of Tora Bora—was their failure to examine and intervene in the affairs of the military. The manner in which these two civilian leaders at the top of the chain of command interacted with their military subordinates enabled the unsuccessful results at Tora Bora. As French statesman Georges Clemenceau famously stated, "War is too important to be left to the generals." This axiom would prove prophetic as President Bush and Secretary Rumsfeld failed to concern themselves with the operational affairs at Tora Bora and question, probe, and overrule General Franks's approach that allowed Osama bin Laden and a large contingent of al Qaeda and Taliban operatives to escape into Pakistan.

Two predominant theories characterize the proper relationship between a civilian leader in the chain of command and his military subordinates. According to Samuel Huntington's "normal" theory of civil-military relations, the military should be left as autonomous as possible to assure its political neutrality and professional ability to safeguard national security. Military officers are therefore professional tacticians who plan and manage military operations, and civilian leaders should only provide strategic guidance and then allow the military to determine how to best achieve those goals through the application of force.[65] This approach to civil-military relations has dominated conventional wisdom and informed the way most American presidents have handled their military commanders.

However, if "the political object is the goal, war is the means of reaching it, and means can never be considered in isolation from their purpose," as the nineteenth-century military theorist Carl von Clausewitz wrote, then it is both inappropriate and impossible to draw a clear distinction between policy, strategy, operations, and tactics, and ends and means.[66] In fact, as military historian Eliot Cohen argues, "the Clausewitzian view is incompatible with the doctrine of professionalism codified by the 'normal' theory of civil-military relations."[67] Therefore, Cohen developed an alternative argument about civil-military relations more in harmony with Clausewitz. According to him, civilian leaders should engage in an unequal dialogue with the military at all levels when necessary by questioning, probing, and if needed overruling the advice of their military subordinates. To support this theory, Cohen cites as examples the successful wartime leadership of Abraham Lincoln, Georges Clemenceau, Winston Churchill, and David Ben-Gurion. In his book *Supreme Command,* Cohen pointedly captures the discourse over the proper civil-military relationship. "The former Supreme Allied Commander Atlantic, Admiral Harry Train, wrote in an analysis of the 1982 Falklands War, 'when the duly accountable political leadership assumes the military role of deciding *how* the armed forces will perform their duties, the nation has a problem,'" Cohen writes. "On the contrary, the truth is that when politicians abdicate their role in making those decisions, the nation has a problem."[68] When applied to the first 102 days of Operation Enduring Freedom, these contrasting frameworks for civil-military relations offer important insights into how Osama bin Laden, al Qaeda, and the Taliban survived 2001.

President Bush and Secretary Rumsfeld followed Huntington's "normal" theory of civil-military relations to guide their interactions with the military during the Battle of Tora Bora. While Bush and Rumsfeld played an active role in setting the initial policy and strategy for the U.S. war in Afghanistan, neither involved himself in the operational details of the battle nor questioned General Franks's approach. In defense of both President Bush and the conventional wisdom on civil-military relations, Under Secretary Feith recorded in his memoir:

The suggestion that the *President* should have told Franks which forces—U.S. or foreign—to use for a particular cordon mission reflects a bizarre conception of the relationship between a President and a wartime military commander. It is hard to imagine any President overriding his general's judgment and ordering him to use American forces to "go kill" bin Laden. A president who would do that needs a new commander.[69]

According to Condoleezza Rice and her deputy Stephen Hadley, the White House did not provide guidance for the Battle of Tora Bora, and a decision about reinforcing the commandos at Tora Bora was never posed to the president. "Some people contend that we had a chance to capture or kill him [Osama bin Laden] at Tora Bora in the waning stages of the initial Afghan campaign in 2001. In fact, there were conflicting reports about his whereabouts at the time, and as a result the military did not request additional forces to conduct a strike," Rice wrote. "To my knowledge, the President was never asked to make a decision about a possible operation. But one thing is certain: if we had known where bin Laden was, we would have done absolutely everything in our power to take him down."[70] Hadley elaborated:

> We didn't get into the details of the operation [the Battle of Tora Bora] but Secretary Rumsfeld and the chairman of the Joint Chiefs did report at least weekly on the operations that were going on in Afghanistan. It was certainly something of which the president was aware, that there was a fight going on in Tora Bora. . . . I can't remember the president ever starting to suggest the forces to be used and how the forces should be positioned in advance of a particular battle. . . . I don't remember any discussion like that [about utilizing different tactics for the Battle of Tora Bora from other previous operations in Afghanistan]. I wouldn't have expected it. That's an issue of tactics, the kind of thing that is best left to the local commander.[71]

The top-level officials at the Defense Department and Central Intelligence Agency were also detached from the operation at Tora Bora and in hindsight remain skeptical that additional U.S. forces would have influenced the outcome. "I never saw requests for more U.S. troops for Tora Bora," Feith recalled.

"Given the topography—extraordinarily high mountains, numerous narrow passes, thousands of caves, some of which are interconnected—it was not at all clear that even if you had thirty thousand additional troops you could cordon the area off and prevent an individual's escape. The idea that you could have prevented a guy with an understanding of that terrain from escaping is just speculation, and not persuasive."[72] Deputy CIA Director John McLaughlin concurred with Feith's perspective:

> I kind of defer to Gary [Berntsen] on this, but in retrospect, I kind of doubt that eight hundred Rangers would have made a big difference. Looking at the length of that border and the terrain, it's a maybe. But I think it has always struck me as a bit of a stretch to say if only we had had that, we would have caught bin Laden. Now, I wasn't there on the ground so I am not entirely confident of my view. . . . I agree that it would have increased the chances, but I am skeptical of the view that we somehow threw away a certain chance to get him.[73]

Furthermore, Rumsfeld had limited operational decisions to the formal chain of command, thus bypassing even the top tier of Defense Department and White House officials. Important decisions on operations in Afghanistan were often discussed privately by him and General Franks. "Rumsfeld ran the Pentagon in a way that strictly protected his unique authority in the chain of command: he did not want anybody in the Pentagon to be interfering with the chain of command regarding war plans and war operations by the combatant commands," Feith observed. "He was the only Defense Department civilian in the chain of command. He would seek the input that he wanted from his staff, but he didn't want multiple sources giving CENTCOM ideas that looked like directives or orders. Those came only from himself."[74] By strictly controlling and forcing information vertically, Rumsfeld ensured that he alone could provide guidance to the military commanders and develop a complete picture of the war effort.

As the top two civilians in the chain of command, both President Bush and Secretary Rumsfeld remained aloof from tactics in general and the progression of events at Tora Bora in particular. Rice later recorded in her memoir that Bush "tended to accept the military's representations—not unquestioningly, but with fewer probes than he would make later in his presidency."[75] Although they asked questions of General Franks at some points over the duration of the fourteen-day battle, neither Bush nor Rumsfeld asked for details of the operation, established an unequal dialogue where Franks's opinion was treated as advice instead of authority, nor provided strategic guidance to Franks that would clarify and direct the tactics and operational approach to the Battle of Tora Bora.

Indeed, how could an engaged president and secretary of defense—who questioned and prodded the military commander about the significant battles being waged in the present, the location of Osama bin Laden, the possibility for his escape, the whereabouts of concentrations of al Qaeda forces in Afghanistan, the reliability of the Eastern Alliance, the potentialities and contingencies, the "knowns and unknowns," and the tactics utilized by American forces—allow a battle for the existence of al Qaeda to be waged by ninety-three Western commandos and a contingent of generally untrustworthy Afghan rebels in bin Laden's suspected hideout without any assurances that a reliable force would seal the escape routes?

Years later, the memoirs of President Bush and Secretary of Defense Rumsfeld confirm their distance from the Battle of Tora Bora in the context of civil-military relations. According to Rumsfeld,

> I was prepared to authorize the deployment of more American troops into the region [Tora Bora] if the commanders requested them. . . . I believed a decision of this nature, which hinged on numerous operational details, was best made by the military commander in charge. Franks had to determine whether attempting to apprehend one man on the run, whose whereabouts were not known with certainty, was worth the risks inherent to such a venture. . . . I made it clear to Franks that if he believed he needed more troops, he would get them as quickly as possible. . . . I never received such a request from either Franks or Tenet and cannot imagine denying it if I had. If someone thought bin Laden was cornered, as later claimed, I found it surprising that Tenet had never called me to urge Franks to support their operation. I can only presume that either their chain of command was not engaged or they failed to convince Tenet of the quality of their information.[76]

Bush also largely deferred to his subordinates and failed to ask the questions to challenge the authority of their advice. In his memoir, he states:

Years later, critics charged that we allowed bin Laden to slip the noose at Tora Bora. I sure didn't see it that way. I asked our commanders and CIA officials about bin Laden frequently. They were working around the clock to locate him, and they assured me that they had the troop levels and resources they need. If we had ever known for sure where he was, we would have moved heaven and earth to bring him to justice.[77]

Despite Rumsfeld's reputation for being a compulsive micromanager, he essentially abdicated all responsibilities surrounding the Battle of Tora Bora, deferring unconditionally to Franks likely without probing him enough to engage the situation at hand. Rumsfeld's distance from this important battle was uncharacteristic. At the start of military operations in October 2001, Rumsfeld generated the "ten days of hell" for CENTCOM by relentlessly questioning the delays in inserting special operations forces into Afghanistan. But at the critical point in the campaign, he had largely withdrawn from overseeing military operations in Afghanistan. It is likely that Rumsfeld was not fully aware of the importance of Tora Bora, partially because he was not receiving an accurate view of the battle from his uniformed subordinates. General Franks was confident in his operational approach to Tora Bora and was therefore unlikely to volunteer to the secretary of defense doubts that he did not share. Also, the battle may not have captured Rumsfeld's attention simply because Franks was not closely overseeing the operation. Nevertheless, Rumsfeld must have had some awareness of the intelligence on bin Laden's presence at Tora Bora but apparently was reluctant to examine the issue and intervene.

The civilian leadership in the Bush administration not only failed to monitor the strategy and operations in Afghanistan but also neglected to provide clear goals and priorities to the military in the first place. Despite the implicit desire to destroy al Qaeda and kill bin Laden, U.S. objectives for the war focused on toppling the Taliban and removing Afghanistan as a haven for terrorists. The confusion and incongruity surrounding American objectives for Afghanistan manifested itself in the Battle of Tora Bora, and nobody responsible for overseeing the implementation of U.S. policy intervened to rectify the situation.

In the end, between President George W. Bush, Secretary of Defense Donald Rumsfeld, National Security Advisor Condoleezza Rice, CIA Director George Tenet, Deputy National Security Advisor Stephen Hadley, and Under Secretary of Defense for Policy Douglas Feith, none of these national leaders were directly engaged in the most important operation of the war. The American leadership succeeded in toppling the Taliban and driving al Qaeda out of Afghanistan. But Osama bin Laden, al Qaeda, and the Taliban survived 2001. In this sense, they had all failed.

It is conceivable, however, that the president and secretary of defense were aware of the request for additional troops for the Battle of Tora Bora. Two isolated accounts of the White House deliberations during the battle tell an alternative story. Journalist Ron Suskind describes in his book how Hank Crumpton briefed the president in late November on the inability of Afghan and Pakistani forces to prevent bin Laden's escape.[78] Suskind further reports that Bush received numerous reports in early December indicating that "the back door was open" for bin Laden at Tora Bora.[79] Similarly, according to Gary Berntsen, Crumpton requested eight hundred Rangers for the battle at a White House meeting in the presence of President Bush, Vice President Cheney, Defense Secretary Rumsfeld, and CIA Director Tenet.[80] Berntsen asserts that the White House eclipsed General Franks in deciding whether or not to reinforce U.S. troops at Tora Bora. Although Berntsen does not reveal his source, he implies that he acquired this information from Crumpton. Berntsen later recalled:

> My understanding is that Hank made the request [for eight hundred Rangers] directly. Secretary Rumsfeld said, "No, the Pakistani Frontier Force is going to cover the back side." And the vice president agreed with him. And the president said nothing. George Tenet said nothing as well. . . . The point is, they knew of the request. . . . Franks and Dailey, my belief was, were just saluting and following orders. . . .
>
> I found out later that he [Crumpton] took it to the White House. . . . That's what I was told, actually, from a very good source. . . . I was angry at the time at Dailey and at Franks for this because I thought that they were not supporting me, only to learn later that the decision was made at the White House.[81]

Crumpton later clarified:

I spoke with General Tommy Franks, CENTCOM Commander, about the need for more American forces at Tora Bora within hours of the request from my men in Afghanistan. . . . I do not know if he spoke with the president, secretary of defense, or others about my request.

Several days earlier I did have a conversation with President Bush in the Oval Office about the possibility of enemy leadership escaping into Pakistan. I showed him maps of the area with possible escape routes, explaining that it would be impossible to seal that border although I noted that more recon/interdiction forces would be helpful. We provided our best intelligence, including confirmation of UBL's presence, and offered our best recommendation but this was ultimately a military decision.[82]

Providing that President Bush and Secretary Rumsfeld were directly approached with the request for eight hundred Rangers, as Berntsen claims, such an account could alter the explanation of how Osama bin Laden escaped Tora Bora. If accurate, General Franks may be absolved from some responsibility for the tactical failure to reinforce the ninety-three U.S. commandos at Tora Bora. Still, Franks neglected to provide sound military advice and defend it before his superiors. And even if the decision reached Bush and Rumsfeld, their failure to examine the situation, question the details, intervene in the affairs of the military, and discover the inadequacy of the established approach confirms their disengagement from the task at hand. Without further corroboration, this alternative narrative remains an interesting but solitary account based on hearsay and unverifiable evidence.[83]

The extent to which Pakistan and the ISI assisted Taliban and al Qaeda operatives in escaping U.S. and Eastern Alliance forces remains the ultimate enigma in the Battle of Tora Bora. Fragmentary and inconclusive evidence suggests that Pakistan played a significant role in shepherding Taliban fighters out of Tora Bora and might have provided similar support to some members of al Qaeda. The evidence is circumstantial and may be erroneous or deceptive. Nonetheless, given the ISI's extensive ties with the Taliban and al Qaeda before 9/11 and its continued subversive activities afterward, a plausible narrative can be constructed to chronicle ISI involvement in the escape of Taliban and al

Qaeda operatives from Tora Bora. Despite significant uncertainty over Pakistan's role, some level of duplicity at Tora Bora would not represent a divergence from Pakistan's ten years of strategic ambiguity after 9/11.

It is not hard to surmise how the ISI could have orchestrated and supported the exodus from Tora Bora. The JeM attack on the Indian Parliament on December 13, 2001, unmistakably assisted al Qaeda and the Taliban in escaping the American and Pakistani dragnets by diverting Pakistani forces from the border. Top-level Indian officials have provided damning evidence linking the ISI to the JeM assault, and it is certainly possible that the ISI directed the JeM to undertake the operation.[84] Whether or not the ISI intended to assist al Qaeda and the Taliban or had some other motive remains a mystery. The level within the Pakistani government at which these actions were sanctioned—if at all—also is unclear. According to Bruce Riedel, "Musharraf privately told our Ambassador in Pakistan at the time that it [the JeM attack on the Indian Parliament] was a very 'dirty' business but never clarified what he meant."[85]

Other evidence supports the theory that the ISI helped America's enemies escape from Tora Bora. Dalton Fury recalls in his memoir how an Afghan fighter supposedly observed a Pakistani helicopter landing on December 1 in the Wazir Valley, the valley immediately to the west of the battleground.[86] Recent testimony from Fida Muhammad, an ISI civilian incarcerated in an Afghan jail, describes a full-fledged ISI operation to escort militants out of Tora Bora and into Pakistan. Journalist Dexter Filkins interviewed Muhammad in early 2011:

> Muhammad told me that his most memorable job came in December, 2001, when he was part of a large I.S.I. operation intended to help jihadi fighters escape from Tora Bora—the mountainous region where bin Laden was trapped for several weeks, until he mysteriously slipped away. Muhammad said that when the American bombing of Tora Bora began, in late November, he and other I.S.I. operatives had gone there, and into other parts of eastern Afghanistan, to evacuate training camps whose occupants included Al Qaeda fighters.
>
> "We told them, 'Shave your beards, change your clothes, and follow us,'" Muhammad said. "We led them to the border with Pakistan and told them they were on their own. And then we went back for more."

Muhammad was part of a four-man team, and there were dozens of such teams. He estimated that the I.S.I. teams evacuated as many as fifteen hundred militants from Tora Bora and other camps: "Not only Arabs but Pakistanis, Uzbeks, and Chechens. I didn't see bin Laden. But there were so many Arabs." The operation had been sanctioned at the highest levels of the I.S.I. "There are people in the I.S.I. who believe the militants are valuable assets," he said. (The I.S.I. denied Muhammad's account.)[87]

Fida Muhammad made it clear to Filkins that this was not just an attempt to exfiltrate Pakistanis but rather a concerted campaign to evacuate everyone, including al Qaeda, from the camps. Speaking of his interview with Muhammad, Filkins later stated:

> The substance of the Tora Bora evacuation was very detailed, and it was very clear, and it made a lot of sense. . . . He said, "I was ordered to go up there and get people out . . . before the bombing, during the bombing, and after the bombing." . . . His instructions were to go to the camps and to get the people out and get them across the border. . . . I gave him every chance to tell me something not as dramatic as what he told me. . . . I was very specific about that. I said, "Did the Arabs just go along for the ride?" And he was like, "No. Our instructions were to get everybody." . . .
>
> The implications are interesting but they are not that surprising. In the sense that we know that there were tons of Pakistanis training in those camps, there were ISI people in those camps. We knew that there was an evacuation from Kunduz, and we know that there were lots of bad guys who got on the planes in that case. So in some ways it is kind of consistent with everything else they were doing. . . .
>
> From my perspective, the guy [Fida Muhammad] was extremely credible.[88]

Many of the top U.S. government officials in 2001 were aware of Pakistan's duplicity even if the extent of double-dealing was unclear. According to Under Secretary Feith:

People understood that the Taliban were the hedging strategy for the ISI. The general perception, I think, was that Musharraf had switched sides and was helping America against the Taliban. But it was clear when there were Defense Department bilateral meetings with the Pakistanis that they were much more willing to say bad things about al Qaeda than about the Taliban. It was clear that the Pakistanis had never completely renounced their hedging strategy of working with the Taliban. We were never completely confident that the ISI was doing the right thing. There were always suspicions that they were hedging. . . .

We were aware that there was a problem. When I met with Musharraf, I would tell him that we had reports of Pakistani support for terrorists or tolerance of terrorists and that these reports were a problem for Pakistan. Musharraf would say they are false. We would respond that it was important that there should be no support or tolerance of this kind. "If the reports are false, it's important that you work with our people to convince them that they are mistaken," I would say. I personally had these conversations with Musharraf, and I assume that Rumsfeld did too. . . .

We did not have great options for dealing with this problem. The Pakistanis were cooperating with us in important ways. One of the ways we responded to the disturbing reports was to say that there were additional forms of cooperation we wanted to have with Pakistan, but we couldn't have them because of the reports that Pakistan was working with terrorist groups. But we couldn't afford to break relations with the Pakistani government while it was playing such an important role in supporting U.S. operations in Afghanistan. Pakistan cooperated with us in some ways and was doing some bad things at the same time.[89]

John McLaughlin, the deputy director of the CIA, offered a similar perspective of Pakistan:

We were quite aware that this was a partner with conflicting interests and that, in the end, the only thing that really matters to you is will they help you achieve the things that you need to achieve, understanding that there may be some unintended consequences of that but believing at the same time that the thing you are going to achieve outweighs that unintended consequence. That's the judgment you are always making. That's, I think, our attitude toward the Pakistanis at that point. . . . Was there a back door there that we worried about? You bet.[90]

In the end, there is too little evidence to state with authority that Pakistan facilitated the evacuation of the Taliban and al Qaeda from Tora Bora. Nonetheless, it certainly lies within the realm of possibility. While Gary Berntsen did not corroborate Fida Muhammad's testimony, he did not dispute it and "had no doubt" that the ISI embarked on such a campaign.[91] The ISI has continuously supported Islamist militants in the region for thirty years, from the Soviet invasion of Afghanistan to the present day. Given that the ISI's institutional momentum heavily favored the Taliban in December 2001, some degree of double-dealing by mid- or high-level intelligence officers would fit both the available evidence and the ISI's established pattern of support for jihadist organizations.

Fury and his special operations team left Tora Bora on December 19. After the exodus of fighters into Pakistan, few al Qaeda elements remained. ODA 561 arrived the next day to help search the now abandoned cave complexes. The Eastern Alliance declared victory. To them, expelling the Taliban and al Qaeda translated into newfound political power. Many in the military, whose mission had been to support the Eastern Alliance in displacing al Qaeda and the Taliban, also viewed the battle as a success.[92] But the failure in leadership, the improper strategic priorities, the reliance on untrustworthy Afghan tribes, the absence of sufficient American troops, Pakistan's inability to seal the border, the military's aversion to risk, and the distraction of Iraq all dampened what had been a tremendously successful war effort.

At a ceremony in Kabul on December 22, Hamid Karzai was sworn in as the prime minister of the Afghan Interim Authority. As General Franks left Karzai's inauguration, his mind drifted to the Western commandos and Hazrat Ali's fighters as they "were closing in on the enemy in the Tora Bora region."[93] To most Western observers, the war appeared to be a resounding success. The United States of America overthrew the Taliban and unsettled al Qaeda in the historical "graveyard of empires" with only a few hundred American troops and CIA officers backed by American airpower. Despite Rumsfeld's flaws, it appeared that he had transformed the military. In 102 days of war, the United

States of America had accomplished every aspect of its strategy in Afghanistan except for what should have been its central policy objective. Bin Laden and al Qaeda lived to see another day.

CONCLUSION

The failures of the Battle of Tora Bora were indicative of the limiting factors on Operation Enduring Freedom from September 11 to December 22, 2001. The aversion to risk within the U.S. military and civilian leadership led the U.S. government to underresource the most important battle of the war while relying on disreputable Afghan tribes to fight the critical aspects of the campaign and Pakistan's Frontier Force to seal the southern border. The civilian leadership in the White House never clearly distinguished between removing Afghanistan as a haven for terrorist organizations and destroying al Qaeda and its leadership. This lack of clarity over objectives ensured that operations were designed only to expel al Qaeda from Afghanistan even when American forces faced an opportunity to decimate and decapitate the terrorist organization. Furthermore, Iraq diverted the attention of the senior military and civilian leadership responsible for planning and executing the war in Afghanistan at its most urgent juncture. Operationally, American forces never lost a battle against al Qaeda. But strategically they never attained victory.

On the other hand, the American strategy in Afghanistan proved remarkably effective in removing the Taliban regime from power. Although indeterminate strategic guidance delayed the effort, the pieces of the campaign ultimately fell into place. Once the joint interagency teams attached to Afghan resistance forces and the U.S. airpower switched from bombing strategic targets to close air support, the Northern Alliance conquered half of Afghanistan in less than two weeks. America skillfully avoided triggering widespread resistance to the war by harnessing the largely organic resistance movement led by the Afghan opposition to the Taliban.

The 102 days of war in Afghanistan represented a time of great successes and even greater possibilities. America swiftly toppled the Taliban and vanquished al Qaeda from the best sanctuary it ever had. But as al Qaeda continues to endure across the world, those 102 days of war are increasingly the stories not of valiant efforts, but of missed opportunities.

EPILOGUE

December 16, 2001 to May 2, 2011

Osama bin Laden evaded American detection for nearly nine years after the Battle of Tora Bora. However, in August 2010, CIA Director Leon Panetta briefed President Barack Obama on a promising piece of intelligence that would ultimately end the most extensive manhunt in history. The CIA had identified bin Laden's suspected courier, a Kuwaiti-born Pakistani named Abu Ahmed al-Kuwaiti who, according to journalist Ahmed Rashid, "had been with Bin Laden since the battle of Tora Bora in 2001."[1] The Agency tracked al-Kuwaiti to a three-story compound in the Bilal Town neighborhood of Abbottabad, a small town thirty miles north of Islamabad and the location of the Pakistan Military Academy. Intelligence officers quickly noted irregularities: the residents burned their trash, the relatively upscale house had no Internet or cable connection, and the structural elements of the house were clearly designed to prevent anyone from seeing a mysterious inhabitant of the third floor, who never left the house except to pace in the courtyard. The CIA became increasingly confident that the compound housed a significant al Qaeda leader, possibly even bin Laden. Indeed, the U.S. government employee who had spent the longest time tracking bin Laden after September 11, a career CIA analyst whose middle name is John, was 80 percent confident that the Abbottabad compound contained Osama bin Laden.[2]

As intelligence collection efforts intensified, President Obama directed his national security team to develop options for a military strike on the Abbottabad compound. On March 14, 2011, he convened the first of five NSC meetings to discuss potential operations against bin Laden's suspected hideout. The standard, low-risk option entailed dropping thirty-two two-thousand-pound guided bombs from B-2 stealth aircraft. While this choice did not necessitate infiltrating American soldiers into Pakistan, the amount of ordnance required to flatten the compound would, according to Vice Chairman of the Joint Chiefs of Staff Gen. James Cartwright, simulate an earthquake in the urban area surrounding the target. A drone strike timed to coincide with the inhabitant's daily walk in the courtyard was also considered. The third major option consisted of a covert helicopter raid using special operations forces to assault the compound. While this riskier option involved both violating Pakistani sovereignty and putting U.S. soldiers thirty miles from the Pakistani capital, the advantages were clear: the helicopter raid ensured that the U.S. government could quickly identify all the residents in the compound, collect valuable intelligence found at the site, and leave with plausible deniability if no al Qaeda member was discovered or no one was home during the raid. While the president did not make a final decision at that point, he instructed his military subordinates to continue developing and begin rehearsing the helicopter raid.[3]

Over the month of April, commandos prepared to enact the operation at the president's behest. On April 10, two dozen Navy SEALs deployed to North Carolina for five days of rehearsals on a replica of the Abbottabad compound.[4] On April 18, the team flew to Nevada to practice the assault along a flight route of similar distance and elevation to the aerial path from Jalalabad, Afghanistan, to Abbottabad. After numerous repetitions and iterations, the SEAL team finalized the operational plan. The operation would be relatively routine aside from its target and location deep inside Pakistan. Twelve SEALs in the first modified Black Hawk helicopter would fly 150 miles from a U.S. base in Jalalabad to Abbottabad and rappel into the front yard of bin Laden's compound. The remaining dozen commandos in the second helicopter would descend onto the roof of the house. Upon arrival, the SEALs would clear the compound of resistance, search the house for bin Laden, collect intelligence, and promptly return to Jalalabad. On April 26, awaiting the president's decision, the SEAL team departed for Jalalabad.[5]

President Obama convened the final national security council meeting to discuss the Abbottabad operation on the afternoon of April 28, 2011. The evidence that indicated bin Laden's presence in Abbottabad was circumstantial and inconclusive. The president later told the news program *60 Minutes,*

At the end of the day, this was still a 55/45 situation. I mean, we could not say definitively that bin Laden was there. Had he not been there, then there would have been significant consequences. Obviously, we're going into the sovereign territory of another country and landing helicopters and conducting a military operation. . . . So there were risks involved geopolitically in making the decision.[6]

The cabinet was divided over the raid. Given the nature of the evidence, some preferred the B-2 bomb strike to the helicopter raid. Others suggested delaying a strike until better intelligence clarified whether bin Laden was at the compound. The president concluded the meeting and indicated that he would soon make a decision. Obama gave the green light the following morning. Due to weather conditions, the operation would take place two days later. The president concluded, "This was the best evidence that we had regarding bin Laden's whereabouts since Tora Bora."[7]

On the cloudless and moonless night of May 1, 2011—just like the start of military operations in October 2001—two stealth Black Hawk helicopters carrying twenty-three Navy SEALs left Jalalabad and flew due east toward Pakistan. Four MH-47 Chinook helicopters departed forty-five minutes later carrying backup teams and fuel in case the main force encountered difficulties. Keeping their rotors spinning, two of the Chinooks landed in a dry riverbed in northwest Pakistan while the other two landed on the Afghan side of the border. Ninety minutes after taking off from Jalalabad, the two Black Hawks veered southeast and approached their target in Abbottabad. An RQ-170 Sentinel stealth drone loitered high above the compound, relaying live video footage of the impending assault to Washington. In the White House Situation Room, President Obama joined his closest national security advisors to watch the operation unfold.[8]

Upon reaching the Abbottabad compound, the first Black Hawk helicopter began to descend above the front yard when it encountered technical difficulties. The tall concrete walls of the compound combined with the powerful turbulence from the chopper to create a downward vortex that forced the helicopter toward the ground. The team had not encountered this problem during rehearsals because the courtyard walls of the replica were constructed with chain-link fences that did not trap air in the same manner as concrete walls.

Additionally, the unexpectedly warm temperatures at Abbottabad may have reduced the air density enough to decrease the amount of lift that the helicopter could generate, thus forcing the chopper into a rapid descent. The commandos braced for impact as the pilot crash-landed in an open area inside the compound. Observing this precipitous and unplanned descent, the pilot of the second helicopter decided against hovering above the roof of the compound and instead landed across the street. The mishap triggered a distress call to the support teams in the Chinooks.[9]

The commando teams had nonetheless prepared for contingencies and soon readjusted their assault. Using C-4 explosive charges, the SEALs breached a series of walls and fortified doors. The assaulting force encountered resistance upon reaching the inner courtyard that contained the main house and guesthouse. SEALs shot and killed Abu Ahmed al-Kuwaiti, the courier who unknowingly had led the CIA to Abbottabad, as he exited the guesthouse with an AK-47. Al-Kuwaiti's brother Abrar and his unarmed wife were also shot at the entrance of the main house.[10] SEALs then entered the house and continued up the stairs upon which they confronted and shot Khalid bin Laden, one of Osama's adult sons. Due to varying accounts of this event, it is unclear whether Khalid was armed and fired at the U.S. soldiers. At the top of the stairs, three SEALs turned right into a hallway when the lead operator observed a tall man with a beard glance out of a bedroom. The lead SEAL quickly entered the bedroom. Two of bin Laden's wives stood ready to accost the SEAL, and one began to charge toward him. The SEAL shot the charging woman in the leg and then wrapped himself around the two wives to protect his teammates in case the two women were wearing explosive vests. The second SEAL entered the bedroom and fired one shot into the chest of Osama bin Laden and a second shot above his left eye. Soon afterward, the voice of the SEAL, using the code word indicating that Osama bin Laden had been found, resonated across the secure radio bands. "For God and country—Geronimo, Geronimo, Geronimo. Geronimo E.K.I.A. [enemy killed in action]."[11]

It was the end; Osama bin Laden was finally dead. But what could explain how in the aftermath of the devastation of September 11 terrorist attacks, the Bush administration failed to kill Osama bin Laden when he was knowingly surrounded at Tora Bora while, on the other hand, the Obama administration succeeded in killing him after inheriting a cold trail? In December 2001, the Bush administration had credible, multisource intelligence indicating that Osama bin Laden had retreated to Tora Bora and was trapped between U.S. forces and the Eastern Alliance. In fact, the intelligence community had pinpointed bin Laden's location to ten meters on the evening of December 10, 2001.[12] Ninety-three U.S. commandos were located within a couple miles of bin Laden's location, and a few thousand more U.S. troops were ready to deploy to his position on a moment's notice. Nonetheless, bin Laden managed to escape Tora Bora and vanish into Pakistan. When President Obama took office in January 2009, the U.S. intelligence community conjectured that bin Laden resided in Pakistan but had no actionable intelligence as to his location. Two and a half years later, President Obama ordered a risky and ultimately successful raid based on inconclusive evidence suggesting that Osama bin Laden resided in a room on the third floor of a compound in Abbottabad, Pakistan.

The comparison between the Battle of Tora Bora and the Abbottabad operation reveals important insights into the role of the president in war. Nevertheless, the circumstances that President Bush confronted during the Battle of Tora Bora were considerably different from those that President Obama faced in the run-up to the Abbottabad raid. In 2001 Bush led a nation and a government in shock and unexpectedly thrust into war. The president and his national security team were forced to respond to a set of events for which they were vastly unprepared. As commander in chief, he subsequently supervised the invasion of a foreign country along with a broader global war on terrorism during a time of extreme uncertainty and fear. He initiated significant reforms to homeland security, intelligence, foreign policy, and national security, all while continuing the regular yet immense responsibilities of the presidency. It was, without question, an extraordinarily difficult moment for President George W. Bush. The Battle of Tora Bora—itself a dynamic and ephemeral event—took place within this challenging context. In contrast, the Abbottabad operation was planned during a stable and routine time of the Obama presidency. Furthermore, time favored President Obama. Unlike the situation at Tora Bora in 2001, when events necessitated a rapid response, Obama had the time to proceed through a deliberate and composed decision-making process.

Despite these differences, presidential leadership and civil-military relations likely played a salient—if not decisive—role in killing Osama bin Laden.

Unlike President Bush, who remained aloof from the Battle of Tora Bora and deferred responsibility to Secretary Rumsfeld and his military subordinates, President Obama engaged in U.S. government efforts to kill bin Laden at all levels. In mid-2009 he wrote to Panetta and directed him to develop a "detailed operational plan" to find Osama bin Laden.[13] As Obama recalled,

> Shortly after I got into office, I brought Leon Panetta privately into the Oval Office and I said to him, "We need to redouble our efforts in hunting bin Laden down. And I want us to start putting more resources, more focus, and more urgency into that mission."[14]

According to Panetta, Obama instructed him to make Osama bin Laden his top priority.[15] While the degree to which these presidential directives affected CIA operations remains unclear, it nonetheless demonstrated the extent to which the president had elevated the issue.

President Obama's active command and deep involvement in the planning process for the Abbottabad operation is unmistakable. The operational plan developed by the military called for a dozen SEALs in each of the two Black Hawk helicopters. But in a rare instance of a president imposing tactics and specifying operational details, Obama ordered the military to deploy four additional helicopters—the MH-47 Chinooks—to provide support in case the operation went awry. These reinforcements included twenty-five additional SEALs and refueling capabilities for the Black Hawk helicopters. The president was concerned that Pakistan would respond militarily if it detected the U.S. incursion, and the reinforcements that he specified ensured that the commandos could "fight their way out of Pakistan" if necessary.[16]

President Obama's directives would prove prescient. The support helicopters that he deployed in the Abbottabad raid may have made the difference between a successful operation and a fiasco. While the Black Hawk crash represented a blip in the assault, it certainly had the potential to become a disastrous setback. A standard UH-60 Black Hawk is designed to transport eleven fully equipped soldiers.[17] Although the operation utilized stealth variants of Black Hawk helicopters, there is no evidence to suggest that these versions have a substantially different capacity from their standard counterpart. After the crash, the lone operable Black Hawk at Abbottabad could not have transported twice its capacity in troops back to Afghanistan in one trip. Therefore, without reinforcements, the SEALs on the ground in Abbottabad had no way to exfiltrate themselves from the perilous situation without additional helicopters. Furthermore, the return flight to Jalalabad was delayed an additional twenty-five minutes when the remaining Black Hawk helicopter rendezvoused with another MH-47 Chinook inside Pakistan to refuel.[18] In the end, the support helicopters turned out to be essential to the completion of the mission and the safety of the American troops.

It is not difficult to imagine how the lack of support helicopters could have led to a drastically different outcome in Abbottabad. Under the best-case scenario where a rescue helicopter would have been ready and waiting at Jalalabad, the ninety-minute flight would have left one dozen SEALs in Abbottabad for at least another forty-five minutes. However, a more plausible scenario entails Pakistani security forces responding to reports of a downed helicopter less than one mile from the Pakistani Military Academy and discovering a contingent of American troops deep inside Pakistani territory. It is hard to know whether a firefight between the Pakistani military and bogged-down SEALs or the death of Osama bin Laden would have had larger repercussions for U.S. security.

In terms of civil-military relations, President Obama's involvement in the affairs of the military was clearly in line with the actions of Lincoln, Clemenceau, Churchill, and Ben-Gurion. Unlike President Bush, who passively relegated the Battle of Tora Bora to Secretary Rumsfeld and General Franks, Obama exhibited successful wartime leadership by exerting authority over the Abbottabad operation at all levels. While Bush did not provide guidance to his subordinates on how to execute the Battle of Tora Bora, Obama dictated the details of the Abbottabad raid down to the number of helicopters. In the two months leading up to the helicopter raid, Obama chaired at least five NSC meetings to discuss and shape the Abbottabad operation.[19] The critical elements of the operation to kill Osama bin Laden in 2011 were determined not at CENTCOM headquarters in Tampa or headquarters in Fort Bragg, but rather at the White House in the presence of the president. Elevating the importance of killing bin Laden within the U.S. government to the presidential level ensured that operational errors like the Battle of Tora Bora would not be repeated.

Three days after the Abbottabad raid, Barack Obama reflected in a television interview for *60 Minutes* on his level of involvement in the planning of the operation:

[I was] about as active [in the planning of the Abbottabad raid] as any project that I've been involved with since I've been President. Obviously we have extraordinary guys. Our special [operations] forces are the best of the best. And so I was not involved in designing the initial plan. But each iteration of that plan they'd bring back to me. Make a full presentation. We would ask questions.

We had multiple meetings in the Situation Room in which we would map out—and we would actually have a model of the compound and discuss how this operation might proceed, and what various options there were because there was more than one way in which we might go about this.

And in some ways sending in choppers and actually putting our guys on the ground entailed some greater risks than some other options. I thought it was important, though, for us to be able to say that we'd definitely got the guy. We thought that it was important for us to be able to exploit potential information that was on the ground in the compound if it did turn out to be him.

We thought that it was important for us not only to protect the lives of our guys, but also to try to minimize collateral damage in the region because this was in a residential neighborhood.[20]

A senior defense official, speaking on background, corroborated the president's active involvement in the Abbottabad raid:

The president's role in this should not be underestimated. I think there was a body of intelligence that was brought forward to him and his team, as was described, but in the final weeks and really months of this, his personal interest and direction and attention pushed the case to a new level that enabled real action. And I think that role is quite important.[21]

Again, it is not entirely appropriate to compare civil-military relations in the Bush administration during the Battle of Tora Bora to civil-military relations in the Obama administration during the Abbottabad raid without recognizing the differences. The nine and a half years that separated these two operations gave the Obama administration a significant advantage in terms of understanding the nature of al Qaeda and Osama bin Laden. In addition to the dynamic Battle of Tora Bora—in comparison to the static target in 2011—the Bush administration in 2001 did not fully comprehend the extent to which al Qaeda depended on bin Laden. Furthermore, operating deep inside Pakistan entailed violating the sovereignty of an ally and therefore necessitated presidential approval. While the Battle of Tora Bora was a part of Operation Enduring Freedom, the Abbottabad raid represented a single covert operation. It is unsurprising, therefore, that President Obama played some role in the development of the raid, even if that role was exceptional. Nonetheless, the differences between these two situations highlight the degree to which President Bush remained detached from the attempts to kill or capture Osama bin Laden in late 2001. His subordinates did not inform him of the significance of the Battle of Tora Bora, and the president made no apparent effort to understand it. Given this contrast, it is clearer than ever that President Bush failed to probe his national security team on the progress toward killing or capturing bin Laden.

Ultimately, the manner in which George W. Bush and Barack Obama interacted with their military subordinates shaped the outcomes of their operations to kill or capture Osama bin Laden. President Bush's and Secretary Rumsfeld's absent role in the Battle of Tora Bora ensured bin Laden's escape, while President Obama's active involvement in the Abbottabad raid prevented the operation from going awry. The evidence delineating the exact role of Obama in planning the Abbottabad operation remains sparse; future historical scholarship with better sources and a more complete understanding of the internal White House deliberations will test the previous claims. Nonetheless, less than two years after those two Black Hawks surreptitiously entered Pakistani airspace on the way to Abbottabad, no better explanation exists for why President Obama succeeded in killing Osama bin Laden and why President Bush failed.

ACKNOWLEDGMENTS

I owe a great deal to the many individuals who helped me in this undertaking. It was an honor and a privilege to write the first iterations of this book under the supervision of two renowned military historians. Dr. Richard Kohn and Dr. Wayne Lee have supported my research at every step of the process. This book was conceptualized during Dr. Kohn's graduate seminar in military history at the University of North Carolina at Chapel Hill. He graciously put me in touch with some of the individuals that I interviewed, while pushing me to reach a new level of critical thinking in class. As my honors thesis advisor, Dr. Lee was the ideal guide to imposing order on chaos. His supervision and instruction has been an invaluable resource on which I have relied. Both are incredible mentors and instructors, and their support and advice was invaluable throughout the process.

I would like to thank Condoleezza Rice, Stephen Hadley, John McLaughlin, Douglas Feith, Gen. Richard Myers, Gen. James Mattis, Lt. Gen. John Mulholland, Amb. Richard Armitage, Amb. James Dobbins, Amb. Zalmay Khalilzad, Gary Berntsen, "Dalton Fury," Steve Coll, Michael Scheuer, and Dexter Filkins for speaking to me on the record. Most were top-level government officials who generously offered their time and opinions to a young college student. They are dedicated public servants who served their country during its most challenging and dangerous days since the Cuban Missile Crisis. I have the highest respect for these individuals and could not be more appreciative of their contribution to my research. I would also like to thank Amb. David Litt, Amb. Ron Neumann, Doug Frantz, Rye Barcott, Bruce Riedel, and Peter Feaver for helping me reach some of these individuals and setting up interviews. Thanks to the following individuals for reading and providing feedback on this book at various stages in its completion: Matthew Asada, Jim DeHart, David Ellison, Kathleen Ellison, Richard Kohn, Wayne Lee, David Litt, Roger Lotchin, Bruce Riedel, Florian Schaub, and Naomi Zeskind. A grant from the Johnston Center for Undergraduate Excellence of the University of North Carolina partially supported travel expenses for interviews.

I am profoundly grateful to Hilary Claggett, Kathryn Owens, and Potomac Books for providing me with this extraordinary opportunity to publish my research. I also would like to express my deep appreciation to Bruce Riedel for writing the foreword. A special word of gratitude goes to Rye Barcott who, in addition to being a great mentor and friend, volunteered to be my agent in all dealings with Potomac Books.

I would also like to thank my family and friends for their continued support. My mother, Naomi Zeskind, has been the best parent that I could ask for. No words can express my appreciation for everything that she has done to make my life better. And finally, my deepest gratitude goes to Kathleen Ellison for her unconditional love and support. She read and edited more versions of my book than anyone else. She has always encouraged me to be a better person and to strive for excellence, and I am most indebted to her.

SOURCES AND METHODOLOGY

The following section discusses in detail the sources and methodology behind 102 Days of War. *Readers interested in understanding the structure of this book may find this convention of historical analysis valuable.*

More than a decade has passed since the first 102 days of Operation Enduring Freedom. Historical understanding is incomplete, largely because almost all of the relevant government documents remain classified. This restriction on sources forces the occasional reliance on a single narrative, usually constructed by an individual privileged by participation or special personal access. I have tried to provide corroborating evidence to such accounts wherever possible and verify salient points with interviewees. In the absence of official documents, I have relied upon a variety of personal memoirs by top American leaders as well as an assortment of secondary sources, military histories, and analytical publications. In addition to written sources, I have interviewed some of the most important participants in planning and executing the first 102 days of OEF. All interviews occurred on the record unless cited otherwise. In instances when sources conflict, I cite the discrepancy and postulate the most likely scenario suggested by the evidence at hand. Because many of the relevant memoirs are polemical and biased, I sought to extract as much factual information as possible and then use the opinionated works as a reflection of the individual's viewpoint.

Bob Woodward's *Bush at War* provides the best available account of the policy-planning process in the White House from September 11, 2001, to the fall of Kabul to the Northern Alliance on November 12, 2001. Former Deputy Secretary of State Richard Armitage told me, "We were encouraged by the administration to talk to Woodward for his first two books [*Bush at War* and *Plan of Attack*]."[1] Armitage, Deputy CIA Director John McLaughlin, and National Security Advisor Condoleezza Rice confirmed specific parts of Woodward's narrative during my interviews with them. President George W. Bush was interviewed twice on the record for *Bush at War*. Although Woodward interviewed more than one hundred people and examined the notes of over fifty NSC meetings, most of his information was obtained on background, preventing the attribution of information to a specific source or sources.[2] Furthermore, Woodward may also have an inherent bias to portray his sources positively, as they continued to provide intimate details about the highest levels of government for his subsequent books.[3]

A significant amount of evidence came from the memoirs and biographies of top American officials whose actions and personalities influenced the outcomes of the opening campaign of OEF. Each provided important insights into the policymaking process through unique if sometimes polemical prisms. Few accepted responsibility for their own mistakes, although they regularly pointed out their colleagues' errors. It was therefore much more useful to use these memoirs to characterize and contextualize an individual by the opinions of his or her colleagues and not primarily from an autobiographical perspective. These memoirs dealt mostly with the process of going to war in Iraq; Afghanistan was typically relegated to a perfunctory chapter or two. Success or failure in Iraq seemed like the dominant issue, and Afghanistan was not subjected to the same level of analysis or scrutiny.

The memoirs of Gen. Tommy Franks, Gen. Hugh Shelton, Gen. Richard Myers, and Lt. Gen. Michael DeLong cover the first 102 days of OEF in some detail and are excellent windows into the views of the military. They are particularly useful in discerning the relationship between White House deliberations and subsequent strategy. While General Franks's memoir almost completely ignores the Battle of Tora Bora, it reveals his personality, thought processes, and attitudes during much of the opening campaign. George Tenet's memoir, *At the Center of the Storm*, highlights the CIA's unusual role in planning and executing a large military campaign. Tenet also provides a lot of information on the president's thinking, objectives, and strategy. Bradley Graham's biography of Donald Rumsfeld and Karen DeYoung's biography of Colin Powell also provide important information about OEF, albeit one degree removed.[4]

134

Douglas Feith's memoir contains the most comprehensive account of the policy-planning process of any senior official in the Bush administration. Feith dedicates more than a hundred pages to the development of the war strategy for Afghanistan and addresses many major themes. Vice President Richard Cheney's and Secretary of Defense Donald Rumsfeld's memoirs include fairly perfunctory sections on Afghanistan. Cheney offers little of substantive value in his discussion of Afghanistan. While Rumsfeld briefly addresses Tora Bora, his comments are revealing. He also released online a selected assortment of previously classified documents that are particularly useful in capturing the internal deliberations following 9/11.[5] Condoleezza Rice's memoir provides an alternative and equally valuable perspective to the narrative that Donald Rumsfeld recorded in his book. The memoir of George W. Bush offers another window into the thoughts and memories of the commander in chief during the start of Operation Enduring Freedom.[6]

At the tactical and operational level, there are three memoirs that are fundamental to establishing a timeline of events and connecting those events to the deliberations in the White House. Gary Schroen, the leader of the first team in Afghanistan, covers in his book *First In* the initial joint operations. In late October, the role of top CIA commander in Afghanistan passed from Schroen to Gary Berntsen. Berntsen's memoir, *Jawbreaker*, covers the critical time period from the shift to close air support of the Northern Alliance to the Battle of Tora Bora. Berntsen convincingly argues that more U.S. troops were necessary to succeed at the Battle of Tora Bora, and he details his unsuccessful requests to add eight hundred Rangers to the battle. The top special operations commander at Tora Bora, using the pen name Dalton Fury, wrote an in-depth account of his time as the operational leader of the Battle of Tora Bora in his memoir *Kill bin Laden*. Fury places the blame for bin Laden's escape on the Eastern Alliance, claiming that even a more conventional approach would not have offered much improvement. Until more documents are declassified, these three books are the foundation for identifying and understanding the operations that took place in Afghanistan from September 11 to December 22, 2001.[7]

In addition to these basic primary sources, a few detailed narratives of varying quality have emerged. Basing his research on dozens of relevant interviews, Doug Stanton offers in *Horse Soldiers* the best description of the battle for

Mazar-i-Sharif. For the Battle of Tora Bora, Peter Bergen's article in the *New Republic* is the most concise and compelling account. Bergen argues that military risk aversion, the reliance on dubious Afghan allies, and the distraction of Iraq culminated in the failure to capture bin Laden. Ahmed Rashid's *Taliban* is one of the best and only accounts of the Taliban written before September 11, while *Descent into Chaos* has a succinct but useful narrative on the beginning of Operation Enduring Freedom. Rashid's latest book, *Pakistan on the Brink*, also offers new details on bin Laden during his time in Abbottabad. Despite its political context and slant, the Senate Foreign Relations Committee report *Tora Bora Revisited: How We Failed to Get Bin Laden and Why It Matters Today* also provides important information and analysis on the Battle of Tora Bora. The report supports Bergen's perspective on Tora Bora, arguing that more U.S. troops could have provided a substantially better chance of capturing or killing bin Laden. Peter Krause, wrote an article titled "The Last Good Chance: A Reassessment of U.S. Operations at Tora Bora" that is quite possibly the best analysis of how bin Laden's escape at Tora Bora could have been prevented. Krause develops and describes what a military plan to cordon off and clear Tora Bora might have looked like and then methodically assesses its feasibility. He argues that this alternative plan would have been the best available option to capture or kill bin Laden given the logistical and geographic constraints.[8]

The official U.S. military histories provide excellent tactical information about OEF even if their coverage and analysis of Tora Bora is negligible and sometimes flawed. Only the 2008 SOCOM history gives adequate consideration to the importance of this battle; the U.S. Army Special Operations Command history of Operation Enduring Freedom, titled *Weapon of Choice,* dedicates less than four of its four hundred pages to Tora Bora. Furthermore, these official histories tend to support the Franks/DeLong perspective of the battle, blaming the Afghan allies for the failure without considering U.S. military actions that could have prevented or challenged bin Laden's escape. *Al Qaeda's Great Escape: The Military and the Media on Terror's Trail* by Philip Smucker is a unique and fascinating account of the Battle of Tora Bora by a journalist who was near the battle for its entirety, yet it is fundamentally flawed due to its lack of any citations or references. Smucker relies on a variety of interviews conducted around Tora Bora to conclude that bin Laden escaped in early December. I am particularly wary of using any information from Smucker's book because many of his assertions are not supported by evidence or documentation and contradict numerous other sources.[9]

Most of the academic debates about the opening campaign of OEF have focused on the so-called Revolution in Military Affairs (RMA) and the viability of the "Afghan Model."[10] In a thoroughly researched monograph titled *Afghanistan and the Future of Warfare*, Stephen Biddle argues that the Afghan Model was neither "a fluke nor . . . a military revolution, but rather . . . a surprisingly orthodox example of modern joint theater warfare—albeit one with unusually heavy fire support for ourselves and our allies."[11] Biddle contends that the Afghan Model succeeded not because of local idiosyncrasies in Afghanistan, but because it was properly applied under the appropriate conditions. Michael O'Hanlon's article in *Foreign Affairs* titled "A Flawed Masterpiece" argues that Operation Enduring Freedom was a masterpiece of strategy that was flawed in its application to Tora Bora. Nonetheless, O'Hanlon argues that the Afghan campaign has significant lessons for the future of U.S. warfare.[12] Max Boot considers the Afghan Model indicative of "the new American way of war."[13] In "Winning the Allies: The Strategic Value of the Afghan Model," Richard Andres, Craig Wills, and Thomas Griffith Jr. argue that the Afghan Model can be used elsewhere to accomplish U.S. national security objectives. Yet this analysis is based partially on a flawed interpretation of the Battle of Tora Bora, combined with a highly optimistic view of the Afghan Model. Indeed, they claim that "the objectives for the Afghans laid out by U.S. war planners were so difficult that even a highly motivated, well-trained, and well-equipped modern army would have had trouble accomplishing them."[14] In contrast, the evidence suggests that sealing off Tora Bora and capturing or killing most enemies was certainly feasible. Krause's article demonstrates the viability of a block-and-sweep maneuver to seal off Tora Bora. And, in an interview, Gen. James Mattis agreed in theory.[15]

Rather than assess whether or not OEF represented a new way of war, this book situates the campaign within the context of institutional processes and civil-military relations in the White House and the Pentagon in the fall of 2001. Arising from this combination of personalities and institutional structures, policies were devised and continuously revised in the days after 9/11. *102 Days of War* describes those structures, personalities, and processes, and then links them to the specific operational outcomes in Afghanistan, culminating in

Osama bin Laden's escape at Tora Bora. Any analysis that fails to examine inputs, process, and outcomes can only offer an incomplete view at best. Looming over these first days of war is the failure of American forces to capture or kill bin Laden. There is no simple, pithy explanation for this dereliction. Rather, this analysis connects the pivotal decisions and tactical events that enabled bin Laden's escape to the broader context of the tactics, operations, strategy, and objectives of the war.

In this regard, the complex interplay of people, precedent, and institutions that define civil-military relations in the United States at any given moment provides an appropriate framework for understanding the factors that culminated in the failure at Tora Bora. Eliot Cohen's *Supreme Command* forms the basis of the civil-military relations analysis. He argues that the successful wartime civilian leaders are the ones who carefully oversee and occasionally direct even the most minute affairs of the military as necessary. This principle provides a framework for understanding the failures of Tora Bora above the operational level.[16] Cohen's examination of how presidents should relate to their military subordinates is in direct contrast to Samuel Huntington's normal theory of civil-military relations, which states that the military should be granted the maximum autonomy in military operations.[17]

As with all books, *102 Days of War* is a product of its sources. No account of this time period can be definitive without access to the official documents that, at time of publication, remain classified. Nevertheless, this book has made extensive use of the available sources and contributes new evidence to the historical record. It is but one step in the interminable process of examining historical events. It may be fifty years before a complete understanding of what happened after 9/11 emerges, but time will ultimately put this book to the test.

NOTES

Preface

1 Sun Tzu, *The Art of Warfare*, trans. Roger Ames (New York: Ballantine Books, 1993), 103.

Introduction

1 Bradley Graham, *By His Own Rules: The Ambitions, Successes, and Ultimate Failures of Donald Rumsfeld* (New York: PublicAffairs, 2009), 307.

2 See Max Boot, "The New American Way of War," *Foreign Affairs*, July/August 2003; Richard Andres, Craig Wills, and Thomas Griffith Jr., "Winning the Allies: The Strategic Value of the Afghan Model," *International Security* 30, no. 3 (Winter 2005/2006).

3 See Peter Bergen, "The Battle for Tora Bora," *New Republic*, December 22, 2009; Committee on Foreign Relations, United States Senate, *Tora Bora Revisited: How We Failed to Get Bin Laden and Why It Matters Today* (Washington: Government Printing Office, 2009).

1: The Lion's Den

1 Lawrence Wright, *The Looming Tower: Al-Qaeda and the Road to 9/11* (New York: Vintage, 2007), 129.

2 Steve Coll, *Ghost Wars: The Secret History of the CIA, Afghanistan, and bin Laden, from the Soviet Invasion to September 10, 2001* (New York: Penguin, 2004), 38–42. Quote from page 40.

3 Ibid., 49–50.

4 Ibid., 51.

5 Ibid., 58.

6 Ibid., 60–70.

7 Peter L. Bergen, *The Osama bin Laden I Know: An Oral History of al-Qaeda's Leader* (New York: Free Press, 2006), 49–73.

8 Wright, *Looming Tower*, 116–17.

9 Ibid., 117–29; Bergen, *Osama bin Laden*, 54–55.

10 For descriptions of the Battle of Jaji, see Bergen, *Osama bin Laden*, 50–57; Wright, *Looming Tower*, 128–38.

11 Coll, *Ghost Wars*, 180.

12 Ibid., 170–86.

13 Ibid., 235–37.

14 Ahmed Rashid, *Descent into Chaos: The U.S. and the Disaster in Pakistan, Afghanistan, and Central Asia* (New York: Penguin, 2009), 11–12.

15 Ahmed Rashid, *Taliban: Militant Islam, Oil, and Fundamentalism in Central Asia* (New Haven, CT: Yale University Press, 2000), 17–28; Rashid, *Descent into Chaos*, 14.

16 Rashid, *Taliban*, 28–29.

17 Ibid., 29.

18 Ibid., 29–40.

19 Ibid., 48–51.

20 Ibid., 50–51.

21 Ibid., 41–54; Rashid, *Descent into Chaos*, 14–15; Coll, *Ghost Wars*, 280–300.

22 Coll, *Ghost Wars*, 293.

23 Wright, *Looming Tower*, 165–83.

24 Ibid., 186.

25 Ibid., 186–203, 218, 221–25.

26 Ibid., 249–53.

27 Roy Gutman, *How We Missed the Story: Osama bin Laden, the Taliban, and the Hijacking of Afghanistan* (Washington: United States Institute of Peace, 2008), 89.

28 National Commission on Terrorist Acts upon the United States, *The 9/11 Commission Report* (Boston: Norton, 2004), 65; Bruce Riedel, *Deadly Embrace: Pakistan, America, and the Future of the Global Jihad* (Washington: Brookings Institution Press, 2011), 55; Gutman, *How We Missed the Story*, 89–90.

29 National Commission, *9/11 Commission Report*, 64–65.

30 Gutman, *How We Missed the Story*, 92.

31 Ibid., 91–92; Riedel, *Deadly Embrace*, 56.

32 Wright, *Looming Tower*, 265–66.

33 Osama bin Laden, "Declaration of War against the Americans Occupying the Land of the Two Holy Places," PBS, http://www.pbs.org/newshour/terrorism/international /fatwa_1996.html.

34 Wright, *Looming Tower*, 278.

35 Osama bin Laden, interview with CNN, March 1997, http://www.youtube.com /watch?v=1F-GUQr4u8Q.

36 Wright, *Looming Tower*, 281.

37 Ibid., 278–81.

38 Ibid., 284–96.

39 "Text of World Islamic Front's Statement Urging Jihad against Jews and Crusaders," Investigative Project, http://www.investigativeproject.org/documents/misc/180.pdf.

40 Coll, *Ghost Wars*, 341; Wright, *Looming Tower*, 294–300.

41 Coll, *Ghost Wars*, 319–20; Wright, *Looming Tower*, 274–77.

42 Coll, *Ghost Wars*, 371–96.

43 Wright, *The Looming Tower*, 311. According to Wright, "The investigators were stunned to learn that nearly a year earlier an Egyptian member of al-Qaeda had walked into the U.S. Embassy in Nairobi and told the CIA about the bombing plot. The agency had dismissed this intelligence as unreliable."

44 Ibid., 403–4; Wright, *Looming Tower*, 306–9, 311.

45 Coll, *Ghost Wars*, 409–11; Wright, *Looming Tower*, 319–20.

46 Riedel, *Deadly Embrace*, 51; Rashid, *Descent into Chaos*, 16, 113; Richard Clarke, *Against All Enemies: Inside America's War on Terror* (New York: Free Press, 2004), 189; Dexter Filkins, "The Journalist and the Spies," *New Yorker*, September 19, 2011.

47 "TIR [Redacted]/Veteran Afghanistan Traveler's Analysis of al Qaeda and Taliban Exploitable Weaknesses," Department of Defense, October 3, 2001; Riedel, *Deadly Embrace*, 51.

48 Clarke, *Against All Enemies*, 189.

49 Coll, *Ghost Wars*, 416–37; Wright, *Looming Tower*, 309–17, 323–24.

50 Wright, *Looming Tower*, 325–27.

51 Rashid, *Descent into Chaos*, 15–19.

52 Ibid., 17.

53 Coll, *Ghost Wars*, 440.

54 See Coll, *Ghost Wars*, 537–39; Wright, *Looming Tower*, 374; Rashid, *Descent into Chaos*, 17–18.

55 Resolution 1333, United Nations Security Council, December 19, 2000; Rashid, *Descent into Chaos*, 18.

56 National Commission, *9/11 Commission Report*, 259.

57 Coll, *Ghost Wars*, 566–68.

58 Ibid., 569.

59 National Commission, *9/11 Commission Report*, 277.

2: Scrambling to Respond

1 Condoleezza Rice, *No Higher Honor: A Memoir of My Years in Washington* (New York: Crown, 2011), 79.

2 For a detailed narrative of the events on the morning of September 11, 2001, see National Commission, *9/11 Commission Report*, 278–323.

3 For a description of Card notifying President Bush of the attacks, see Bob Woodward, *Bush at War* (New York: Simon & Schuster, 2002), 15–16.

4 Department of Defense, *2001 Quadrennial Defense Review* Report, iv.

5 Ibid., iv, 8.

6 For a narrative of Rumsfeld's actions on the morning of September 11, 2001, see Graham, *By His Own Rules*, 281–84. For a description of the Quadrennial Defense Review, see http://www.defense.gov/QDR/.

7 George Tenet, *At the Center of the Storm: My Years at the CIA* (New York: HarperCollins, 2007), 161–69.

8 Karen DeYoung, *Soldier: The Life of Colin Powell* (New York: Knopf, 2006), 338–41.

9 For the location of bin Laden on September 11, 2001, see Committee on Foreign Relations, *Tora Bora Revisited*; Wright, *Looming Tower*, 417.

10 Coll, *Ghost Wars*, 582.

11 Ibid., 107–24.

12 Rashid, *Descent into Chaos*, 11–12.

13 "Text of Bush's Address," CNN, September 11, 2001, http://archives.cnn.com/2001/US/09/11/bush.speech.text.

14 For a brief description of the military preparations for Afghanistan before September 11, 2001, see Richard Myers, *Eyes on the Horizon: Serving on the Front Lines of*

National Security (New York: Threshold, 2009), 166; Tommy Franks, *American Soldier* (New York: Regan Books, 2004), 250.

15 Myers, *Eyes on the Horizon*, 140.

16 Michael Scheuer, interview by author, March 30, 2010.

17 Tenet, *At the Center of the Storm*, 208.

18 For the CIA's experience and preparations in Afghanistan before September 11, 2001, see Tenet, *At the Center of the Storm*, 171; National Commission, *9/11 Commission Report*, 108–43; Coll, *Ghost Wars*, 89–186; Wright, *Looming Tower*, 297–375.

19 Douglas Feith, *War and Decision: Inside the Pentagon at the Dawn of the War on Terrorism* (New York: HarperCollins, 2008), 48.

20 Ibid., 49.

21 Ibid., 50.

22 Ibid., 48–50. Quote from page 50.

23 Douglas Feith, interview by author, January 25, 2012.

24 John McLaughlin, interview by author, January 26, 2012.

25 Woodward, *Bush at War*, 52.

26 Tenet, *At the Center of the Storm*, 176.

27 For a description of the NSC meeting, see Woodward, *Bush at War*, 50–53; Tenet, *At the Center of the Storm*, 175–76.

28 For a narrative of Powell and Armitage's actions on September 13, 2001, see Woodward, *Bush at War*, 58–59; Tenet, *At the Center of the Storm*, 179–81; Richard Armitage, interview by author, April 5, 2010.

29 Riedel, *Deadly Embrace*, 45–47, 51–53; Rashid, *Descent into Chaos*, 41–45. Quote from Rashid, *Descent into Chaos*, 44.

30 Pervez Musharraf, *In the Line of Fire: A Memoir* (New York: Free Press, 2006), 201.

31 Armitage, interview.

32 See Woodward, *Bush at War*, 58–59; Tenet, *At the Center of the Storm*, 179–81; Armitage, interview.

33 Tenet, *At the Center of the Storm*, 181.

34 Rashid, *Descent into Chaos*, 28–33.

35 S.J. Res. 23/ PL 107-40, 107th Congress, September 14, 2001.

36 Tenet, *At the Center of the Storm*, 177.

37 Ibid., 178.

38 For a narrative of the CIA presentation at Camp David on September 15–16, 2001, see Tenet, *At the Center of the Storm*, 175–79; Woodward, *Bush at War*, 74–78.

39 Hugh Shelton, *Without Hesitation: The Odyssey of an American Warrior*, with Ronald Levinson and Malcolm McConnell (New York: St. Martin's, 2010), 445.

40 For the military options presented at Camp David on September 15–16, 2001, see Woodward, *Bush at War*, 80; Myers, *Eyes on the Horizon*, 165–67; Shelton, *Without Hesitation*, 443–45.

41 Woodward, *Bush at War*, 80.

42 Ibid., 88.

43 Ibid., 81–91.

44 Woodward, *Bush at War*, 98.

45 Ibid., 81.

46 For the opinions of Powell and Tenet on targeting, see Woodward, *Bush at War*, 87–89. For the actions of the cabinet members mentioned, see Woodward, *Bush at War*, 97–101.

47 Donald Rumsfeld, *Known and Unknown: A Memoir* (New York: Sentinel, 2011), 360.

48 Myers, *Eyes on the Horizon*, 168.

49 Information about Armitage's trip to Moscow from Armitage, interview.

50 Myers, *Eyes on the Horizon*, 164.

3: Preparing for War

1 Berntsen, interview.

2 Gary Schroen, *First In: An Insider's Account of How the CIA Spearheaded the War on Terror in Afghanistan* (New York: Ballantine Books, 2005), 11–38. Quote from page 38.

3 CENTCOM's AOR covered twenty-seven nations spanning from East Africa across the Arabian Peninsula and northeast into Kazakhstan.

4 Myers, *Eyes on the Horizon*, 171–74. Quote from page 174.

5 "Transcript of President Bush's address," CNN, September 20, 2001, http://archives .cnn.com/2001/US/09/20/gen.bush.transcript/.

6 Franks, *American Soldier*, 276.

7 Shelton, *Without Hesitation*, 446.

8 Michael DeLong, *Inside CENTCOM: The Unvarnished Truth about the Wars in Afghanistan and Iraq*, with Noah Lukeman (Washington: Regnery, 2004), 28.

9 For descriptions of the meeting with the service chiefs, including Frank's perspective, see Franks, *American Soldier*, 275–77; DeLong, *Inside CENTCOM*, 27–28.

10 Quote from Franks, *American Soldier*, 280. For a narrative of the briefing with President Bush, see Franks, *American Soldier*, 278–82; Myers, *Eyes on the Horizon*, 176–77.

11 For a description of the CIA field appraisal, see Woodward, *Bush at War*, 121–26. For a description of the meeting, see pages 127–30. Quote from page 128.

12 For the discussion about basing rights in Uzbekistan on September 24, 2001, see ibid., 129–30.

13 Due to a limitation of sources, I have been unable to attribute this decision to specific individuals within the military.

14 James Mattis, interview by author, April 8, 2010.

15 For the delays in implementing CSAR, see Woodward, *Bush at War*, 151–52, 164–65, 179. Quote from page 164.

16 For the challenges in targeting, see Myers, *Eyes on the Horizon*, 179–80; Graham, *By His Own Rules*, 300; Woodward, *Bush at War*, 157–58, 164–65, 174–75. Quotes from Woodward, *Bush at War*, 174.

17 Schroen, *First In*, 73–150.

18 For more information on Schroen's field appraisal, see Schroen, *First In*, 146. For information on the NSC meeting, see Woodward, *Bush at War*, 191–95. The decision to overthrow the Taliban regime was confirmed by Condoleezza Rice in my interview with her on June 30, 2010.

19 Tenet, *At the Center of the Storm*, 180.

20 Information on Mahmud's portrayal of Mullah Omar from McLaughlin, interview.

21 Riedel, *Deadly Embrace,* 66.

22 Zalmay Khalilzad, interview by author, January 26, 2012.

23 Luke Harding, "Taliban Will Not Sacrifice Bin Laden," *The Guardian*, March 30, 2001, http://www.guardian.co.uk/world/2001/mar/31/alqaida.afghanistan ?INTCMP=SRCH; Riedel, *Deadly Embrace,* 56.

24 Tenet, *At the Center of the Storm*, 182–83.

25 Ibid., 210, 214.

26 Woodward, *Bush at War*, 191–95.

27 Berntsen, interview. This remains one of the only available accounts of the plan devised by Franks. Hank Crumpton also offers a similar account of the general plan for the U.S. war in Afghanistan. Henry Crumpton, *The Art of Intelligence: Lessons from a Life in the CIA's Clandestine Service* (New York: Penguin, 2012), 191–93.

28 Berntsen, interview.

29 Ibid.

30 McLaughlin, interview.

31 Rumsfeld, *Known and Unknown*, 370.

32 Feith, *War and Decision*, 63.

33 Rice, *No Higher Honor*, 94–95.

4: A Slow Start

1 Carl von Clausewitz, *On War*, ed. and trans. Michael Howard and Peter Paret (Princeton, NJ: Princeton University Press, 1976), 579.

2 "Presidential Address to the Nation," White House, October 7, 2001, http://georgewbush-whitehouse.archives.gov/news/releases/2001/10/20011007-8.html.

3 George W. Bush, *Decision Points* (New York: Crown, 2010), 184.

4 "Rumsfeld and Myers Briefing on Enduring Freedom," Department of Defense, October 7, 2001. http://www.defense.gov/transcripts/transcript.aspx?transcriptid=2011.

5 Condoleezza Rice, interview by author, June 30, 2010.

6 Stephen Hadley, interview by author, March 3, 2011.

7 Feith, *War and Decision*, 84; Feith, interview.

8 Rumsfeld, *Known and Unknown*, 367.

9 Feith, interview.

10 See Rumsfeld, *Known and Unknown*, 367–70; Feith, *War and Decision*, 75–84.

11 Richard Myers, interview by author, April 9, 2010.

12 DeLong, *Inside CENTCOM*, 36.

13 John Mulholland, interview by author, November 9, 2010.

14 Mattis, interview.

15 Tenet, *At the Center of the Storm*, 178.

16 McLaughlin, interview.

17 Berntsen, interview.

18 Crumpton, *Art of Intelligence*, 177.

19 Armitage, interview.

20 James Dobbins, interview by author, March 29, 2010.

21 For details about the bombing campaign on October 7, 2001, see Schroen, *First In*, 151–56; Woodward, *Bush at War*, 207–12; Franks, *American Soldier*, 283–96; Myers, *Eyes on the Horizon*, 187–88.

22 Woodward, *Bush at War*, 211.

23 For the October 8, 2001 meeting and the ensuing Bomb Damage Assessment, as well as Musharraf's removal of Mahmud, see Woodward, *Bush at War*, 211–13.

24 Rashid, *Descent into Chaos*, 13.

25 Ibid., 3–6, 10, 12–14, 16–17, 19.

26 Schroen, *First In*, 161–64. Quote from page 161.

27 For Franks's account of the "ten days of hell," see Franks, *American Soldier*, 296–301. For the bombing report on October 9, see "DOD News Briefing: Secretary Rumsfeld and General Myers," Department of Defense, October 9, 2001, http://www.defense.gov/transcripts/transcript.aspx?transcriptid=2034.

28 See Franks, *American Soldier*, 296–301; Feith, *War and Decision*, 63–64, 96, 104, 106–7.

29 Feith, interview.

30 "'Rumsfeld's Rules' Find Pentagon Readers," Department of Defense, January 23, 2001.

31 Donald Rumsfeld, "2001-10-10 to Myers Pace re What Will Be the Military Role in the War on Terrorism?," *The Rumsfeld Papers*, www.rumsfeld.com.

32 Schroen, *First In*, 189–205.

5: The Strategic Void

1 Antoine-Henri Jomini, *Traité des grandes operations militaires, contenant l'histoire des campagnes de Frédéric II, compares à celles de l'empereur Napoléon; avec un recueil des principes généraux de l'art de la guerre*, 2:312n. Accessed through John Shy, "Jomini," in *Makers of Modern Strategy: From Machiavelli to the Nuclear Age*, ed. Peter Paret (Princeton, NJ: Princeton University Press, 1986), 146.

2 The following narrative comes primarily from Woodward's *Bush at War*. What we know about the high-level deliberations during this time period is largely due to Woodward's access. Although Woodward does not make this claim, what seems to emerge is a lack of consensus over the future of Kabul and the absence of a strategy for southern Afghanistan.

3 Woodward, *Bush at War*, 213–37.

4 See Schroen, *First In*, 209–16; Myers, *Eyes on the Horizon*, 192; Woodward, *Bush at War*, 249–50; Franks, *American Soldier*, 301–5. Augmented by Myers, interview.

5 Rice, *No Higher Honor*, 92.

6 Woodward, *Bush at War*, 243.

7 Ibid., 242–47.

8 Armitage, interview. Woodward's account of this event indicates that the dialogue was between McLaughlin and Rumsfeld, while Armitage stated that it was between Tenet and Rumsfeld. Condoleezza Rice's *No Higher Honor* mentions that it was McLaughlin who represented the CIA at that meeting. McLaughlin also indicated that he attended the meeting (McLaughlin, interview).

9 McLaughlin, interview.

10 Berntsen, interview.

11 Ibid.

12 For the NSC meetings, see Woodward, *Bush at War*, 250–51. For a description of Fahim's front lines, see Schroen, *First In*, 121–28.

13 Berntsen, interview.

14 For information on the DIA report, see Woodward, *Bush at War*, 268; Tenet, *At the Center of the Storm*, 216–17.

15 Rice, interview.

16 See Woodward, *Bush at War*, 254–63; Bush, *Decision Points*, 199.

17 Berntsen, interview.
18 Schroen, *First In*, 265–69.
19 Ibid., 304–5; Gary Berntsen, with Ralph Pezzullo, *Jawbreaker: The Attack on Bin Laden and Al-Qaeda: A Personal Account by the CIA's Key Field Commander* (New York: Three Rivers, 2006), 88–94.
20 Armitage, interview.
21 Mulholland, interview.
22 Dobbins, interview.
23 Berntsen, interview.
24 Ibid.
25 Crumpton, *Art of Intelligence*, 194.
26 See "2001-9-30 to President Bush re Strategic Thoughts," *The Rumsfeld Papers*, www.rumsfeld.com; "2001-10-30 to Dough Feith re Strategy," *The Rumsfeld Papers*, www.rumsfeld.com; Feith, *War and Decision*, 75–84; Rumsfeld, *Known and Unknown*, 368.
27 Hadley, interview.
28 Rice, interview.
29 Rumsfeld, "2001-10-10 to Myers Pace."

6: Dominoes

 1 "The President's News Conference, April 7, 1954," The American Presidency Project, University of California at Santa Barbara, http://www.presidency.ucsb.edu /ws/index.php?pid=10202.
 2 Doug Stanton, *Horse Soldiers: The Extraordinary Story of a Band of U.S. Soldiers Who Rode to Victory in Afghanistan* (New York: Scribner, 2009), 139–40.
 3 Ibid., 120–44; Charles Briscoe, Richard Kiper, James Schroder, and Kalev Sepp, *Weapon of Choice: U.S. Army Special Operations Forces in Afghanistan* (Fort Leavenworth, KS: Combat Studies Institute Press, 2003), 125–26.
 4 Stanton, *Horse Soldiers*, 142–46; Briscoe et al., *Weapon of Choice*, 125–26; U.S. Air Force, "Fact Sheet: JOINT DIRECT ATTACK MUNITION," http://www.af.mil /information/factsheets/factsheet_print.asp?fsid=108&page=1.
 5 Stanton, *Horse Soldiers*, 142–46; Briscoe et al., *Weapon of Choice*, 125–26.
 6 Rashid, *Taliban*, 56.
 7 Ibid.
 8 Ibid.
 9 Stanton, *Horse Soldiers*, 150–56; Schroen, *First In*, 311–13.
10 Stanton, *Horse Soldiers*, 160–68.
11 For a narrative of the November 2 NSC meeting, see Woodward, *Bush at War*, 287–92.
12 Feith, interview.
13 Stanton, *Horse Soldiers*, 172.
14 According to Briscoe et al., *Weapon of Choice*, 98, ODA 534 inserted on November 4. However, Stanton, *Horse Soldiers*, 193, indicates that this occurred on November 2. Since *Weapon of Choice* is the official account, November 4 is likely the correct date.
15 See Berntsen, *Jawbreaker*, 133–38; Woodward, *Bush at War*, 294–95. For a transcript of the November 6, 2001 press release, see "DOD News Briefing— Secretary Rumsfeld and Gen. Pace," Department of Defense, November 6, 2001, http://www.defense.gov/transcripts/transcript.aspx?transcriptid=2311.

16 Stanton, *Horse Soldiers*, 235–42; Woodward, *Bush at War*, 299.

17 See Berntsen, *Jawbreaker*, 136–39; Woodward, *Bush at War*, 299–302; Stanton, *Horse Soldiers*, 247–66.

18 Berntsen, interview.

19 Ibid.

20 See Committee on Foreign Relations, *Tora Bora Revisited*, 4; Hamid Mir, "Osama Claims He Has Nukes: If US Uses N-arms It Will Get Same Response," November 10, 2001, http://archives.dawn.com/2001/11/10/top1.htm.

21 See Briscoe et al., *Weapon of Choice*, 97–101; Woodward, *Bush at War*, 309.

22 See Berntsen, *Jawbreaker*, 164–82; Woodward, *Bush at War*, 304–11. Quote from Woodward, page 306.

23 Feith, interview.

24 McLaughlin, interview.

25 Berntsen, interview.

26 Woodward, *Bush at War*, 310.

27 Ibid., 311.

28 Berntsen, interview.

29 For Karzai's insertion into Tarin Kowt, see Tenet, *At the Center of the Storm*, 220. Information on the strike that killed Atef and the plan to insert a team into Asadabad comes from my interview with Berntsen.

30 For information on Sayyaf's shift to Jalalabad, see Woodward, *Bush at War*, 310. For bin Laden's location on November 14, 2001, see Bergen, *Osama bin Laden*, 333; Committee on Foreign Relations, *Tora Bora Revisited*, 4; Bergen, "Battle for Tora Bora."

31 Berntsen, interview.

32 National Commission, *9/11 Commission Report*, 65; Riedel, *Deadly Embrace*, 55; Gutman, *How We Missed the Story*, 89–90.

33 Rashid, *Descent into Chaos*, 214.

34 Berntsen, interview.

35 Briscoe et al., *Weapon of Choice*, 155–58.

36 Ibid., 107, 167–71.

37 Rashid, *Descent into Chaos*, 92.

38 Ibid., 91–92; Seymour Hersh, "The Getaway," *New Yorker*, January 28, 2002; Dexter Filkins and Carlotta Gall, "Pakistanis Again Said to Evacuate Allies of Taliban," *New Yorker*, November 24, 2001; Dexter Filkins, interview by author, September 20, 2011. For Major General Qureshi's statement, see "Efforts on for Pakistanis' Evacuation from Kunduz: Violators to Face Legal Action," *Dawn*, November 25, 2001, http://archives.dawn.com/2001/11/25/top5.htm.

39 Berntsen, interview. Amrullah Saleh was a Northern Alliance leader referred to in Berntsen's *Jawbreaker* as "Majid." However, in my interview with Berntsen, he first revealed Majid's true identity.

40 Rashid, *Descent into Chaos*, 92.

41 Feith, interview.

42 Filkins, interview.

43 Hersh, "The Getaway."

44 See Tenet, *At the Center of the Storm*, 221–24; Briscoe et al., *Weapon of Choice*, 158–65; Berntsen, *Jawbreaker*, 245–54.

45 Rashid, *Descent into Chaos*, 93.

46 Berntsen, *Jawbreaker*, 270.
47 Berntsen, interview.
48 Ibid.
49 Dobbins, *After the Taliban: Nation-Building in Afghanistan* (Washington: Potomac Books, 2008), 85.
50 Ibid., 84–85.
51 Department of Defense, "DOD News Briefing: Secretary Rumsfeld and Gen. Franks," November 27, 2001, http://www.defense.gov/transcripts/transcript.aspx ?transcriptid=2465.
52 Scheuer, interview.

7: Distractions

1 Rice, interview.
2 Feith, *War and Decision*, 48.
3 Rice, *No Higher Honor*, 86.
4 Rice, interview.
5 See Graham, *By His Own Rules*, 288–94; Woodward, *Bush at War*, 49, 60–61, 83–85, 91, 99. Quote from Woodward, *Bush at War*, page 99.
6 Myers, *Eyes on the Horizon*, 215.
7 Ibid., 215.
8 See Franks, *American Soldier*, 315; Myers, *Eyes on the Horizon*, 215–17; Graham, *By His Own Rules*, 326–29; Committee on Foreign Relations, "*Tora Bora Revisited*," 12; Bob Woodward, *Plan of Attack* (New York: Simon & Schuster, 2004), 6–8. The Senate Foreign Relations Committee report on Tora Bora incorrectly cites Franks's memoir to claim that this phone call between Rumsfeld and Franks occurred on November 21, 2001. The November 21 conversation on Iraq took place between Rumsfeld and Myers and informally between Maj. Gen. Gene Renuart (Franks's chief of operations [J-3] at CENTCOM) and Lt. Gen. Gregory Newbold (the director of operations [J-3] for the Joint Chiefs of Staff), while the call between Rumsfeld and Franks about OPLAN 1003 occurred six days later on November 27. Bradley Graham in his book *By His Own Rules* also makes this mistake, claiming that Rumsfeld "immediately directed General Tommy Franks to devise a concept of operations" on Iraq on November 21, 2001. But on that date, Renuart informally warned Franks of the impending formal request after Newbold informed Renuart. For this aspect of the line of communication, see Woodward, *Plan of Attack*, 6–8. On page 425 of *Known and Unknown*, Rumsfeld states that the president asked him to review the war plans for Iraq on September 26, just fifteen days after 9/11. There is no evidence to corroborate this claim. A senior government official, speaking off the record, refuted this aspect of Rumsfeld's account.
9 Information on OPLAN 1003 from Woodward, *Plan of Attack*, 8. The Afghan model was "practically untested," since its current use represented the first "test." Because the situation in Afghanistan remained dynamic as of November 27, 2001, an overall judgment on the efficacy of the model could not be adequately made.

8: A Battle Won and a War Lost

1 Clausewitz, *On War*, 582.
2 Bergen, "Battle for Tora Bora"; Committee on Foreign Relations, *Tora Bora Revisited*.

3 Berntsen, interview.

4 Berntsen, *Jawbreaker*, 214.

5 Ibid., 214–15, 225, 239–40, 249–50, 253–54, 256–57, 261–62.

6 Berntsen, interview; Meena Baktash, "Obituary, Abdul Qadir," *The Guardian*, July 7, 2002, http://www.guardian.co.uk/news/2002/jul/08/guardianobituaries .afghanistan; Rod Nordland, "Afghan Warlord with Many Enemies, and Possibly One Notorious Ally, Killed by Suicide Bomber," *New York Times*, February 22, 2010, http://www.nytimes.com/2010/02/23/world/asia/23taliban.html.

7 Berntsen, *Jawbreaker*, 275.

8 Berntsen, interview.

9 Berntsen, *Jawbreaker*, 274–77; Bergen, "Battle for Tora Bora."

10 Crumpton, *Art of Intelligence*, 259.

11 See Berntsen, *Jawbreaker*, 212, 265–74; Briscoe et al., *Weapon of Choice*, 215; Dalton Fury, *Kill bin Laden: A Delta Force Commander's Account of the Hunt for the World's Most Wanted Man* (New York: St. Martin's, 2008), 100; Tenet, *At the Center of the Storm*, 226. Quote from *Jawbreaker*, page 269.

12 Berntsen, interview.

13 Fury, *Kill bin Laden*, 81–82, 100; *History of the United States Special Operations Command*, 6th ed, USSOCOM History and Research, Department of Defense, 2008, 98.

14 Dalton Fury, interview by author, February 8, 2011; Berntsen, interview.

15 Briscoe et al., *Weapon of Choice*, 107–8.

16 Berntsen, *Jawbreaker*, 289–90; Bergen, "Battle for Tora Bora"; Fury, interview.

17 Fury, *Kill bin Laden*, 106–48; Bergen, "Battle for Tora Bora"; *History of the United States Special Operations Command*, 98. Peter Bergen writes that the transfer of command from the CIA to Dalton Fury took place on December 7, while the *History of the United States Special Operations Command* states that this event occurred on December 8.

18 Fury, *Kill bin Laden*, 149–62; Berntsen, *Jawbreaker*, 289–95.

19 Fury, *Kill bin Laden*, 173.

20 Ibid., 166–73, 190.

21 Ibid., 174–86; *History of the United States Special Operations Command*, 99–100. Quote from Fury, *Kill bin Laden*, page 185.

22 Fury, *Kill bin Laden*, 186–210; *History of the United States Special Operations Command*, 99–100.

23 Fury, *Kill bin Laden*, 217.

24 See ibid., 210–27; Bergen, "Battle for Tora Bora"; Committee on Foreign Relations, *Tora Bora Revisited*, 11–12; *History of the United States Special Operations Command*, 100. The Senate Foreign Relations Committee report incorrectly identifies the date of the surrender ordeal. According to Fury's account, the surrender event lasted from December 11 until the 12th, but the scheduled deadline was 8 a.m. on December 13. Army special operations forces prematurely broke the ceasefire at 5 p.m. on December 12 (Fury, page 219). The *History of the United States Special Operations Command* also indicates that the surrender negotiations began on December 11.

25 Bin Laden experienced the victory at Jaji on Leilat al-Qadr in 1987. Because Islam relies on a lunar calendar, Leilat al-Qadr in 2001 did not fall on the same date in the Gregorian calendar as it did in 1987.

26 Fury, *Kill bin Laden*, 233–34.

27 Ibid., 228–40.
28 Bruce Riedel, "How 9/11 Is Connected to December 13," Brookings Institution, September 11, 2008, http://www.brookings.edu/research/opinions/2008/09/11 -terrorism-riedel.
29 Ibid.; Riedel, *Deadly Embrace*, 68–70.
30 See Fury, *Kill bin Laden*, 234–50; Berntsen, *Jawbreaker*, 306–7. There remains some confusion about the last signals intercept of bin Laden speaking through shortwave radio in Tora Bora. On page 307, Berntsen's account states that this communication occurred on the afternoon of December 15, not December 14 as Fury recounts in *Kill bin Laden*.
31 See Fury, *Kill bin Laden*, 250–61; Berntsen, *Jawbreaker*, 307–8.
32 Berntsen, *Jawbreaker*, 307–8. The details of bin Laden's escape—including the exact dates and escape route—remain somewhat unclear. Recent reporting suggests an alternative route out of Tora Bora. Official documents indicate that Osama bin Laden may have traveled northeast from Tora Bora to Kunar Province on horseback. Ron Suskind's book also supports this account (Ron Suskind, *The One Percent Doctrine: Deep inside America's Pursuit of Its Enemies since 9/11* (New York: Simon & Schuster, 2007), 75). While this alternative route is plausible, the evidence remains fragmented at best. The bulk of the evidence still indicates that Osama bin Laden left Tora Bora and traveled southward into Pakistan.
33 Fury, *Kill bin Laden*, 293.
34 See ibid., xxiii, 262–66, 291–93; Myers, *Eyes on the Horizon*, 196; Fury, interview.
35 Bush, *Decision Points*, 202.
36 Scheuer, interview.
37 Fury, interview.
38 Fury, *Kill bin Laden*, 190.
39 Briscoe et al., *Weapon of Choice*, 214.
40 Mulholland, interview.
41 According to Fury, his orders for Tora Bora were issued directly by Dailey (Fury, interview). According to Mulholland, Franks was his boss in the military chain of command and "that's who I took my marching orders from" (Mulholland, interview).
42 Peter John Paul Krause, "The Last Good Chance: A Reassessment of U.S. Operations at Tora Bora," *Security Studies* 17, no. 4 (October 2008): 670.
43 Peter Bergen, *The Longest War: The Enduring Conflict between America and Al-Qaeda* (New York: Free Press, 2011), 73.
44 Fury, interview.
45 See Tenet, *At the Center of the Storm*, 226–27. Quote from page 227.
46 Crumpton, *Art of Intelligence*, 257–58. Quote from page 258.
47 Ibid., 258.
48 Tactically this would not be the appropriate method to seal a border, but the statistic illustrates the point.
49 For troop dispositions in early December, see Bergen, "Battle for Tora Bora"; Briscoe et al., *Weapon of Choice*, 213–16; Mattis, interview; Fury, interview. Quote from Mattis, interview.
50 Fury, interview.
51 Ibid.
52 Berntsen, interview.

53 For a detailed analysis of the logistics of rapidly inserting troops into Tora Bora, see Krause, "Last Good Chance," 644–84.

54 Berntsen, *Jawbreaker*, 238.

55 Berntsen, interview.

56 Fury, interview.

57 See Franks, *American Soldier*, 323–25; Myers, *Eyes on the Horizon*, 193–94; DeLong, *Inside CENTCOM*, 54–57; Graham, *By His Own Rules*, 307–8; Tenet, *At the Center of the Storm*, 226–27; Woodward, *Bush at War*, 155, 310; Bergen, "Battle for Tora Bora"; Committee on Foreign Relations, *Tora Bora Revisited*; Mattis, interview. Quote from Tommy Franks, "War of Words," *New York Times*, October 19, 2004, http://www.nytimes.com/2004/10/19/opinion/19franks.html?scp=1&sq=franks%20bin%20laden%20october%2019,%202004&st=cse.

58 Bush, *Decision Points*, 184.

59 Mulholland, interview.

60 Rumsfeld, *Known and Unknown*, 403.

61 Feith, *War and Decision*, 67.

62 Ibid., 49–50.

63 Woodward, *Bush at War*, 310–11.

64 The mission of these Marines comes from a credible source that provided this information off the record.

65 For the "normal" theory of civil-military relations, see Samuel Huntington, *The Soldier and the State: The Theory and Politics of Civil-Military Relations* (Cambridge, MA: Harvard University Press, 1957), 80–97, 456–66; Eliot Cohen, *Supreme Command: Soldiers, Statesmen, and Leadership in Wartime* (New York: Free Press, 2002), 4–14, 241–64.

66 Clausewitz, *On War*, 87. This argument using Clausewitz's analysis of war comes from Cohen, *Supreme Command*, 4–14.

67 Cohen, *Supreme Command*, 8.

68 Ibid., 1–14, 208–24. Quote from page 14.

69 Feith, *War and Decision*, 136.

70 Rice, *No Higher Honor*, 119.

71 Hadley, interview.

72 Feith, interview.

73 McLaughlin, interview.

74 Feith, interview.

75 Rice, *No Higher Honor*, 96.

76 Rumsfeld, *Known and Unknown*, 402–3.

77 Bush, *Decision Points*, 202.

78 Ron Suskind, *The One Percent Doctrine*, 58–59.

79 Ibid., 74–75.

80 Berntsen, interview.

81 Ibid.

82 Thomas A. Ricks, "Your Questions for Crumpton—and His Answers about Tora Bora, Torture, Cheney, 'Thunderball,' and Good Books on Intel," *Foreign Policy*, June 5, 2012, http://ricks.foreignpolicy.com/posts/2012/06/05/your_questions_for_crumpton_and_his_answers_about_tora_bora_torture_cheney_thunderb.

83 Douglas Feith is skeptical that the request could have occurred in the setting described. According to him, Rumsfeld would have been furious if Crumpton posed an operational question to the president without Rumsfeld and Tenet discussing it first. He speculates, "If Tenet did not make the request to Rumsfeld, then perhaps the problem was that the CIA people on the scene failed to convince Tenet that their views about bin Laden's whereabouts were correct" (Feith, interview). No one to date has provided convincing evidence to confirm or deny Berntsen's account.

84 Riedel, "How 9/11 Is Connected"; Riedel, *Deadly Embrace*, 68–70.

85 Riedel, "How 9/11 Is Connected"; Riedel, *Deadly Embrace*, 68–70. Quote from page 69 of *Deadly Embrace*.

86 Fury, *Kill bin Laden*, 272–73.

87 Filkins, "Journalist and the Spies."

88 Filkins, interview.

89 Feith, interview.

90 McLaughlin, interview.

91 Berntsen, interview.

92 See Fury, *Kill bin Laden*, 263–79; Briscoe et al., *Weapon of Choice*, 213–16.

93 Franks, *American Soldier*, 322.

Epilogue

1 Ahmed Rashid, *Pakistan on the Brink: The Future of America, Pakistan, and Afghanistan* (New York: Viking, 2012), 5.

2 Nicholas Schmidle, "Getting bin Laden," *New Yorker*, August 8, 2011; Eric Schmitt and Thom Shanker, *Counterstrike: The Untold Story of America's Secret Campaign against al Qaeda* (New York: Times Books, 2011), 257–65; "Obama on bin Laden: The Full *60 Minutes* Interview," *CBS News*, May 4, 2011, http://www.cbsnews.com /8301-504803_162-20060530-10391709.html; "Press Briefing by Senior Administration Officials on the Killing of Osama bin Laden"; Adam Goldman and Matt Apuzzo, "Meet 'John': The CIA's bin Laden Hunter-in-Chief," MSNBC, July 5, 2011, http://www.msnbc.msn.com/id/43637044/ns/us_news-security/t/meet -john-cias-bin-laden-hunter-in-chief/.

3 Schmidle, "Getting bin Laden"; Schmitt and Shanker, *Counterstrike*, 257–65; "Press Briefing by Senior Administration Officials on the Killing of Osama bin Laden."

4 Schmidle, "Getting bin Laden." According to Schmidle, "Brian, James, and Mark selected a team of two dozen SEALs . . . and told them to report to a densely forested site in North Carolina for a training exercise on April 10th."

5 Schmidle, "Getting bin Laden"; Bill Sweetman, "Stealth Helos Used in Osama Raid," *Aviation Week*, May 3, 2011; Christopher Drew, "Attack on Bin Laden Used Stealthy Helicopter That Had Been a Secret," *New York Times*, May 5, 2011, http://www.nytimes .com/2011/05/06/world/asia/06helicopter.html; "CIA Chief Panetta: Obama Made 'Gutsy' Decision on Bin Laden Raid," *PBS Newshour*, May 3, 2011.

6 "Obama on bin Laden."

7 Ibid.; Schmidle, "Getting bin Laden." Quote from "Obama on bin Laden."

8 Schmidle, "Getting bin Laden." According to Schmidle, "A video link connected them to Panetta, at C.I.A. headquarters, and McRaven, in Afghanistan. (There were at least two other command centers, one inside the Pentagon and one inside the American Embassy in Islamabad.) Brigadier General Marshall Webb . . . took a seat

at the end of a lacquered table in a small adjoining office and turned on his laptop. He opened multiple chat windows that kept him, and the White House, connected with the other command teams. The office where Webb sat had the only video feed in the White House showing real-time footage of the target, which was being shot by an unarmed RQ 170 drone flying more than fifteen thousand feet above Abbottabad."

9 Ibid.; Schmitt and Shanker, *Counterstrike*, 264–65.

10 Sources differ on the identity of the woman shot. Schmidle's article claims that she was Abrar's wife, while *Counterstrike* indicates that she was Abu Ahmed's wife.

11 Schmidle, "Getting bin Laden"; Schmitt and Shanker, *Counterstrike*, 264–65.

12 Fury, *Kill bin Laden*, 166–73, 190.

13 Schmidle, "Getting bin Laden."

14 "Obama on bin Laden."

15 "Interview with Leon Panetta," *NBC Nightly News*, May 3, 2011.

16 Schmidle, "Getting bin Laden"; Schmitt and Shanker, *Counterstrike*, 262.

17 "Black Hawk Fact File for the United States Army," U.S. Army, http://www.army.mil/factfiles/equipment/aircraft/blackhawk.html.

18 Schmidle, "Getting bin Laden."

19 "Press Briefing by Senior Administration Officials on the Killing of Osama bin Laden."

20 "Obama on bin Laden."

21 "DOD Background Briefing with Senior Defense Officials from the Pentagon and Senior Intelligence Officials by Telephone on U.S. Operations Involving Osama Bin Laden," U.S. Department of Defense, Office of the Assistant Secretary of Defense (Public Affairs), May 2, 2011.

Sources and Methodology

1 Armitage, interview.

2 Woodward, *Bush at War*, xi–xiii.

3 See Woodward's books *Bush at War*, *Plan of Attack*, *State of Denial*, and *The War Within*.

4 Franks, *American Soldier*; Shelton, *Without Hesitation*; Myers, *Eyes on the Horizon*; DeLong, *Inside CentCom*; Tenet, *At the Center of the Storm*; Graham, *By His Own Rules*; DeYoung, *Soldier*.

5 *The Rumsfeld Papers*, www.rumsfeld.com.

6 Feith, *War and Decision*; Richard Cheney and Liz Cheney, *In My Time: A Personal and Political Memoir* (New York: Threshold Editions, 2011); Rumsfeld, *Known and Unknown*; Rice, *No Higher Honor*; Bush, *Decision Points*.

7 Schroen, *First In*; Berntsen, *Jawbreaker*; Fury, *Kill bin Laden*.

8 Stanton, *Horse Soldiers*; Bergen, "Battle for Tora Bora"; Committee on Foreign Relations, *Tora Bora Revisited*; Krause, "Last Good Chance," 644–84.

9 *History of the United States Special Operations Command*; Briscoe et al., *Weapon of Choice*; Philip Smucker, *Al Qaeda's Great Escape: The Military and the Media on Terror's Trail* (Washington: Brassey's, 2004).

10 The "Afghan Model" refers to the use of special operations forces attached to indigenous forces to direct precision-guided munitions and close air support.

11 Stephen Biddle, *Afghanistan and the Future of Warfare: Implications for Army and Defense Policy* (Carlisle, PA: Strategic Studies Institute, 2002), 43. Biddle's

monograph relies primarily on a series of over forty interviews with relevant government officials who took part in the opening campaign of Operation Enduring Freedom in some manner. The interviews are stored at the United States Military History Institute but are classified at the top secret/FOCAL POINT level and thus inaccessible to individuals outside of the special operations community.

12 Michael O'Hanlon, "A Flawed Masterpiece," *Foreign Affairs*, May/June 2002.
13 Boot, "New American Way of War."
14 Andres et al., "Winning the Allies," 145.
15 Krause, "Last Good Chance," 644–84; Mattis, interview.
16 Cohen, *Supreme Command*.
17 Huntington, *Soldier and the State*.

SELECTED BIBLIOGRAPHY

Andres, Richard, Craig Wills, and Thomas Griffith Jr. "Winning the Allies: The Strategic Value of the Afghan Model." *International Security* 30, no. 3 (Winter 2005/2006): 124–60.

Bergen, Peter. "The Battle for Tora Bora." *The New Republic*. December 22, 2009.

———. *The Longest War: The Enduring Conflict between America and Al-Qaeda*. New York: Free Press, 2011.

———. *The Osama bin Laden I Know: An Oral History of al Qaeda's Leader*. New York: Free Press, 2006.

Berntsen, Gary, with Ralph Pezzullo. *Jawbreaker: The Attack on Bin Laden and Al-Qaeda: A Personal Account by the CIA's Key Field Commander*. New York: Three Rivers, 2006.

Biddle, Stephen. *Afghanistan and the Future of Warfare: Implications for Army and Defense Policy*. Carlisle, PA: Strategic Studies Institute, 2002.

bin Laden, Najwa, Omar bin Laden, and Jean P. Sasson. *Growing up Bin Laden: Osama's Wife and Son Take Us inside Their Secret World*. New York: St. Martin's, 2009.

Blaber, Peter. *The Men, the Mission, and Me: Lessons from a Former Delta Force Commander*. New York: Berkley Caliber, 2008.

Blehm, Eric. *The Only Thing Worth Dying For: How Eleven Green Berets Forged a New Afghanistan*. New York: Harper, 2010.

Boot, Max. "The New American Way of War." *Foreign Affairs*. July/August 2003.

Briscoe, Charles, Richard Kiper, James Schroder, and Kalev Sepp. *Weapon of Choice: U.S. Army Special Operations Forces in Afghanistan*. Fort Leavenworth, KS: Combat Studies Institute Press, 2005.

Bush, George W. *Decision Points*. New York: Crown, 2010.

Cheney, Dick, and Liz Cheney. *In My Time: A Personal and Political Memoir*. New York: Threshold Editions, 2011.

Clarke, Richard A. *Against All Enemies: Inside America's War on Terror*. New York: Free Press, 2004.

Clausewitz, Carl von. *On War*. Edited and translated by Michael Howard and Peter Paret. Princeton, NJ: Princeton University Press, 1976.

Cohen, Eliot. *Supreme Command: Soldiers, Statesmen, and Leadership in Wartime*. New York: Free Press, 2002.

Coll, Steve. *The bin Ladens: An Arabian Family in the American Century*. New York: Penguin, 2008.

———. *Ghost Wars: The Secret History of the CIA, Afghanistan, and bin Laden, from the Soviet Invasion to September 10, 2001*. New York: Penguin, 2005.

Committee on Foreign Relations, United States Senate, *Tora Bora Revisited: How We Failed to Get Bin Laden and Why It Matters Today* (Washington: Government Printing Office, 2009).

Corbin, Jane. *Al-Qaeda: In Search of the Terror Network That Threatens the World*. New York: Thunder Mouth Press/Nation Books, 2002.

Crumpton, Henry. *The Art of Intelligence: Lessons from a Life in the CIA's Clandestine Service*. New York: Penguin, 2012.

———. "Intelligence and War: Afghanistan, 2001–2002." In *Transforming US Intelligence*, edited by Jennifer Sims and Burton Gerber. Washington: Georgetown University Press, 2005.

DeLong, Michael. *Inside CENTCOM: The Unvarnished Truth about the Wars in Afghanistan and Iraq*. With Noah Lukeman. Washington: Regnery, 2004.

DeYoung, Karen. *Soldier: The Life of Colin Powell*. New York: Knopf, 2006.

Dobbins, James. *After the Taliban: Nation-Building in Afghanistan*. Washington: Potomac Books, 2008.

Drendel, Lou. *Operation Enduring Freedom: US Military Operations in Afghanistan, 2001–2002*. Carrollton, TX: Squadron/Signal Publications, 2002.

Feith, Douglas. *War and Decision: Inside the Pentagon at the Dawn of the War on Terrorism*. New York: HarperCollins, 2008.

Finlan, Alastair. *Special Forces, Strategy and the War on Terror: Warfare by Other Means*. London: Routledge, 2008.

Franks, Tommy. *American Soldier*. New York: HarperCollins, 2004.

Fury, Dalton. *Kill Bin Laden: A Delta Force Commander's Account of the Hunt for the World's Most Wanted Man.* New York: St. Martin's, 2008.

Graham, Bradley. *By His Own Rules: The Ambitions, Successes, and Ultimate Failures of Donald Rumsfeld.* New York: PublicAffairs, 2009.

Gutman, Roy. *How We Missed the Story: Osama bin Laden, the Taliban, and the Hijacking of Afghanistan.* Washington: United States Institute of Peace, 2008.

History of the United States Special Operations Command, 6th ed. USSOCOM History and Research, Department of Defense, 2008.

Huntington, Samuel. *The Soldier and the State: The Theory and Politics of Civil-Military Relations.* Cambridge, MA: Harvard University Press, 1957.

Jomini, Antoine-Henri. *Traité des grandes operations militaires, contenant l'histoire des campagnes de Frédéric II, compares à celles de l'empereur Napoléon; avec un recueil des principes généraux de l'art de la guerre.* 2d ed., 4 vols. Paris, 1811.

Katzman, Kenneth. *Afghanistan: Post-Taliban Governance, Security, and U.S. Policy.* Washington: Congressional Research Service, 2009.

Krause, Peter John Paul. "The Last Good Chance: A Reassessment of U.S. Operations at Tora Bora." *Security Studies* 17, no. 4 (October 2008): 644–84 (2008).

Lambeth, Benjamin. *Air Power against Terror: America's Conduct of Operation Enduring Freedom.* Santa Monica, CA: Rand, 2005.

Musharraf, Pervez. *In the Line of Fire: A Memoir.* New York: Free Press, 2006.

Myers, Richard E. *Eyes on the Horizon: Serving on the Front Lines of National Security.* New York: Threshold, 2009.

National Commission on Terrorist Attacks upon the United States. *The 9/11 Commission Report.* Boston: Norton, 2004.

Neumann, Ronald. *The Other War: Winning and Losing in Afghanistan.* Washington: Potomac Books, 2009.

O'Hanlon, Michael. "A Flawed Masterpiece." *Foreign Affairs.* May/June 2002.

Olsen, John Andreas. *A History of Air Warfare.* Washington: Potomac Books, 2010.

Paret, Peter, ed. *Makers of Modern Strategy: From Machiavelli to the Nuclear Age.* Princeton, NJ: Princeton University Press, 1986.

Rashid, Ahmed. *Descent into Chaos: The U.S. and the Disaster in Pakistan, Afghanistan, and Central Asia.* New York: Penguin, 2009.

———. *Pakistan on the Brink: The Future of America, Pakistan, and Afghanistan.* New York: Viking, 2012.

———. *Taliban: Militant Islam, Oil and Fundamentalism in Central Asia*. New Haven, CT: Yale University Press, 2000.

Rice, Condoleezza. *No Higher Honor: A Memoir of My Years in Washington*. New York: Crown, 2011.

Riedel, Bruce. *Deadly Embrace: Pakistan, America, and the Future of the Global Jihad*. Washington: Brookings Institution Press, 2011.

Rothstein, Hy. *Afghanistan and the Troubled Future of Unconventional Warfare*. Annapolis, MD: Naval Institute Press, 2006.

Rumsfeld, Donald. *Known and Unknown: A Memoir*. New York: Sentinel, 2011.

Scheuer, Michael. *Imperial Hubris: Why the West Is Losing the War on Terror*. New York: Potomac Books, 2008.

Schmitt, Eric, and Thom Shanker. *Counterstrike: The Untold Story of America's Secret Campaign against al Qaeda*. New York: Times Books, 2011.

Schroen, Gary. *First In: An Insider's Account of How the CIA Spearheaded the War on Terror in Afghanistan*. New York: Ballantine, 2005.

Shelton, Hugh. *Without Hesitation: The Odyssey of an American Warrior*. With Ronald Levinson and Malcolm McConnell. New York: St. Martin's, 2010.

Smucker, Philip. *Al Qaeda's Great Escape: The Military and the Media on Terror's Trail*. Washington: Brassey's, 2004.

Stanton, Doug. *Horse Soldiers: The Extraordinary Story of a Band of U.S. Soldiers Who Rode to Victory in Afghanistan*. New York: Scribner, 2009.

Stewart, Richard W. *Operation Enduring Freedom: The United States Army in Afghanistan, October 2001–March 2002*. CMH Pub 70-83-1. Washington: U.S. Army Center of Military History.

Suskind, Ron. *The One Percent Doctrine: Deep inside America's Pursuit of Its Enemies since 9/11*. New York: Simon & Schuster, 2007.

Tenet, George. *At the Center of the Storm: My Years at the CIA*. New York: HarperCollins, 2007.

Tzu, Sun. *The Art of Warfare*. Translated by Roger Ames. New York: Ballantine, 1993.

Woodward, Bob. *Bush at War*. New York: Simon & Schuster, 2002.

———. *Plan of Attack*. New York: Simon & Schuster, 2004.

Wright, Donald, James Bird, Steven Clay, Peter Connors, Scott Farquhar, Lynn Garcia, and Dennis Wey. *A Different Kind of War*. Fort Leavenworth, KS: Combat Studies Institute Press, 2010.

Wright, Lawrence. *The Looming Tower: Al-Qaeda and the Road to 9/11*. New York: Vintage, 2007.

Interviews

Amb. Richard Armitage—April 5, 2010, telephone

Gary Berntsen—December 16, 2011

Steve Coll—July 28, 2010

Amb. James Dobbins—March 29, 2010, telephone

Douglas Feith—January 25, 2012

Dexter Filkins—September 20, 2011, telephone

"Dalton Fury"—February 8, 2011, e-mail

Stephen Hadley—March 3, 2011, telephone

Amb. Zalmay Khalilzad—January 26, 2012

Gen. James Mattis—April 8, 2010

John McLaughlin—January 26, 2012

Lt. Gen. John Mulholland—November 9, 2010

Gen. Richard Myers—April 9, 2010

Condoleezza Rice—June 30, 2010, mail/fax

Michael Scheuer—March 30, 2010

Amb. Hank Crumpton, Lt. Gen. Dell Dailey, Gen. Tommy Franks, and Gen. Hugh Shelton declined to be interviewed.

INDEX

ABOUT THE AUTHOR

Yaniv Barzilai is a U.S. diplomat. Yaniv graduated with highest honors and highest distinction from the University of North Carolina in 2011 with a BA in Peace, War, and Defense and a minor in Arabic. In 2013, Yaniv received an MA in international relations with honors from the Johns Hopkins School of Advanced International Studies (SAIS), where he concentrated in strategic studies and international economics.

Yaniv has worked for the Special Representative for Afghanistan and Pakistan at the U.S. Department of State in Washington, DC, and the Special Representative for Somalia at the U.S. Embassy in Nairobi, Kenya. He has also worked as a desk officer in the Office of Afghanistan Affairs at the State Department. He was awarded the Thomas R. Pickering Foreign Affairs Fellowship from the U.S. Department of State in 2009.

Yaniv currently lives in Washington, DC, and may be contacted through his website, www.102daysofwar.com.